Quick & Easy
BAKING

CONTENTS

The aroma of a freshly baked cake, the taste of a still warm biscuit and the compliments of family and friends is what *Quick and Easy Baking* is all about.

There are many books about baking, but we have looked at how this rewarding pastime can fit into today's busy lifestyle. We have developed a range of wonderful cakes, cookies and slices that are quick and easy to make – most can be prepared and baked in under an hour.

Each ingredient you use when making these wonderful home baked goodies plays an important role in the finished cake or biscuit so look out for the feature columns telling you about sugar, flour, butter and other ingredients that are essential for making so many of these wonderful recipes. Understanding how they work ensures that you get results that will make you want to bake and bake again.

In the Baker's Kitchen, we have chosen step-by-step recipes to show how easy some of the most complicated looking cakes and biscuits, are to make.

So turn the pages, choose a recipe and start baking, then sit back and wait for the admiration.

Happy Baking

Rachel Blackmore
Food Editor

UK COOKERY EDITOR
Katie Swallow

EDITORIAL
Food Editor: Rachel Blackmore
Assistant Food Editor: Anneka Mitchell
Home Economist: Donna Hay
Recipe Development: Sheryle Eastwood
Editorial Coordinator: Margaret Kelly
Subeditor: Ella Martin

PHOTOGRAPHY
Harm Mol
Ashley Mackevicius (cover)

STYLING
Wendy Berecry

DESIGN AND PRODUCTION
Manager: Nadia Sbisa
Layout: Lulu Dougherty
Finished Art: Stephen Joseph
Cover Design: Frank Pithers

PUBLISHER
Philippa Sandall

© J.B. Fairfax Press Pty Ltd, 1991
This book is copyright. No part may be
reproduced or transmitted by any process
without the written permission of the publishers.

Includes Index
ISBN 1 86343 069 5(pbk)
ISBN 1 85391 224 7

Formatted by J.B. Fairfax Press Pty Ltd
Output by Adtype, Sydney
Printed by Toppan Printing Co, Hong Kong

Distributed by J.B. Fairfax Press Ltd
9 Trinity Centre, Park Farm Estate
Wellingborough, Northants
Ph: (0933) 402330 Fax: (0933) 402234

THE PANTRY SHELF

Unless otherwise stated the following ingredients used in this book are:

Cream   Double, suitable for whipping
Flour   White flour, plain or standard
Sugar   White sugar

WHAT'S IN A TABLESPOON?

NEW ZEALAND
1 tablespoon 15 mL 3 teaspoons
UNITED KINGDOM
1 tablespoon 15 mL 3 teaspoons
AUSTRALIA
1 tablespoon 20 mL 4 teaspoons

The recipes in this book were tested in Australia where a 20 mL tablespoon is standard. All measures are level.

The tablespoon in the New Zealand and United Kingdom sets of measuring spoons is 15 mL. In many recipes this difference will not matter. For recipes using baking powder, gelatine, bicarbonate of soda, small quantities of flour and cornflour, simply add another teaspoon for each tablespoon specified.

CHECK-AND-GO

Use the easy Check-and-Go boxes which appear beside each ingredient. Simply check your pantry and if the ingredients are not there, tick the boxes as a reminder to add those items to your shopping list.

CANNED FOOD

Can sizes vary between countries and manufacturers. You may find the quantities in this book are slightly different from what is available. Purchase and use the can size nearest to the suggested size in the recipe.

CHOCOLATE

For many, chocolate is a delicious obsession. For the Aztecs, who discovered it, chocolate was 'food for the gods'. In its various forms – block chocolate, cocoa powder and chocolate chips, grated, melted and chopped – chocolate is one of the most popular ingredients in cakes, biscuits and slices.

Right: Chocolate Shortbread, Brownies, White Choc-Chip Chocolate Cake (all recipes page 6)

QUICK NUT FUDGE CAKE

Makes a 20 cm/8 in round cake
Oven temperature 180°C, 350°F, Gas 4

- ☐ **125 g/4 oz butter, melted**
- ☐ **1¹/₂ cups/250 g/8 oz soft brown sugar**
- ☐ **2 eggs, lightly beaten**
- ☐ **1 teaspoon vanilla essence**
- ☐ **¹/₄ cup/30 g/1 oz cocoa powder, sifted**
- ☐ **2 cups/250 g/8 oz self-raising flour, sifted**
- ☐ **60 g/2 oz chopped walnuts**

CHOCOLATE BUTTER ICING
- ☐ **125 g/4 oz butter, softened**
- ☐ **100 g/3¹/₂ oz dark chocolate, melted and cooled**
- ☐ **2 egg yolks**
- ☐ **¹/₂ cup/75 g/2¹/₂ oz icing sugar, sifted**

1 Place butter, brown sugar, eggs and vanilla essence in a large mixing bowl and mix to combine. Stir in cocoa powder, flour and walnuts. Mix well to combine.

2 Spoon batter into a greased and lined 20 cm/8 in round cake tin and bake for 35-40 minutes or until cake is cooked when tested with a skewer. Stand cake in tin for 5 minutes before turning onto a wire rack to cool.

3 To make icing, place butter in a mixing bowl and beat until light and fluffy. Add chocolate, egg yolks and icing sugar and beat until smooth. Spread icing over cold cake.

CHOCOLATE SHORTBREAD

*Melt-in-the-mouth
chocolate-flavoured shortbread.*

Makes 30
Oven temperature 160°C, 325°F, Gas 3

- ☐ **250 g/8 oz butter, softened**
- ☐ **¹/₂ cup/75 g/2¹/₂ oz icing sugar**
- ☐ **1 cup/125 g/4 oz flour**
- ☐ **1 cup/125 g/4 oz cornflour**
- ☐ **¹/₄ cup/30 g/1 oz cocoa powder**

1 Place butter and icing sugar in a mixing bowl and beat until mixture is creamy. Sift together flour, cornflour and cocoa powder. Stir flour mixture into butter mixture.

2 Turn dough onto a floured surface and knead lightly until smooth. Roll spoonfuls of mixture into balls, place on greased baking trays and flatten slightly with a fork. Bake for 20-25 minutes or until firm. Allow to cool on trays.

WHITE CHOC-CHIP CHOCOLATE CAKE

A rich chocolate cake studded with white chocolate chips and topped with creamy white chocolate frosting.

Makes a 23 cm/9 in round cake
Oven temperature 180°C, 350°F, Gas 4

- ☐ **125 g/4 oz butter, softened**
- ☐ **1 cup/220 g/7 oz caster sugar**
- ☐ **1 teaspoon vanilla essence**
- ☐ **2 eggs**
- ☐ **1¹/₃ cups/170 g/5¹/₂ oz self-raising flour**
- ☐ **¹/₄ cup/30 g/1 oz cocoa powder**
- ☐ **¹/₂ teaspoon baking powder**
- ☐ **1 cup/250 mL/8 fl oz milk**
- ☐ **200 g/6¹/₂ oz white chocolate, chopped**

WHITE CHOCOLATE FROSTING
- ☐ **125 g/4 oz butter, softened**
- ☐ **100 g/3¹/₂ oz white chocolate, melted and cooled**
- ☐ **2 egg yolks**
- ☐ **¹/₂ cup/75 g/2¹/₂ oz icing sugar, sifted**

1 Place butter, sugar and vanilla essence in a mixing bowl and beat until mixture is creamy. Add eggs one at a time beating well after each addition.

2 Sift together flour, cocoa powder and baking powder. Fold flour mixture and milk, alternately, into butter mixture, then fold in chocolate.

3 Spoon batter into a greased and lined 23 cm/9 in round cake tin and bake for 30-35 minutes or until cooked when tested with a skewer. Stand in tin for 5 minutes before turning onto a wire rack to cool completely.

4 To make frosting, place butter in a mixing bowl and beat until light and fluffy. Add chocolate, egg yolks and icing sugar and beat until smooth. Spread frosting over top and sides of cold cake.

BROWNIES

Makes 25
Oven temperature 180°C, 350°F, Gas 4

- ☐ **155 g/5 oz butter, softened**
- ☐ **¹/₂ cup/170g/5¹/₂ oz honey, warmed**
- ☐ **4 teaspoons water**
- ☐ **2 eggs, lightly beaten**
- ☐ **1³/₄ cups/220 g/7 oz self-raising flour, sifted**
- ☐ **²/₃ cup/125 g/4 oz soft brown sugar**
- ☐ **125 g/4 oz dark chocolate, melted and cooled**
- ☐ **icing sugar**

1 Place butter, honey, water, eggs, flour, sugar and chocolate in a food processor and process until ingredients are combined.

2 Spoon batter into a greased and lined 23 cm/9 in square cake tin and bake for 30-35 minutes or until cooked when tested with a skewer. Stand cake in tin for 5 minutes before turning onto a wire rack to cool. Dust cold cake with icing sugar and cut into squares.

MELTING CHOCOLATE

≈ Chocolate melts more rapidly if broken into small pieces.

≈ The melting process should occur slowly, as chocolate scorches if overheated.

≈ Keep the container in which the chocolate is being melted, uncovered and completely dry. Covering can cause condensation and just one drop of water will ruin the chocolate.

≈ Chocolate 'seizes' if it is overheated or if it comes in contact with water or steam. Seizing results in the chocolate tightening and becoming a thick mass that will not melt.

≈ To rescue seized chocolate stir in a little cream or vegetable oil until the chocolate becomes smooth again.

≈ To melt chocolate, place in a bowl and set aside. Fill a saucepan with enough water to come just under the bowl; the water should not touch the bowl when it is placed in the saucepan. Bring water to the boil, then remove from heat and place chocolate over the hot water. Stand off the heat, stirring occasionally until chocolate melts and is of a smooth consistency. Cool at room temperature.

≈ Chocolate can be melted quickly and easily in the microwave oven. Place chocolate in a microwave-safe glass or ceramic dish and cook on HIGH (100%) for 2 minutes per 375 g/12 oz chocolate. When melting chocolate in the microwave oven you will find that it tends to hold its shape, so always stir it before additional heating. If the chocolate is not completely melted, cook for an extra 30 seconds, then stir again.

Tiles Country Floors Plate and pots Accoutrement Glass jar and wooden rack Butler & Co

DOUBLE-CHOC COOKIES

An old-time favourite. Served with a glass of icy cold milk, what better treat is there.

Makes 30
Oven temperature 180°C, 350°F, Gas 4

☐ **75 g/2^1/$_2$ oz butter, softened**
☐ **^{1}/$_4$ cup/60 g/2 oz caster sugar**
☐ **1^1/$_4$ cups/155 g/5 oz flour**
☐ **^{1}/$_4$ cup/30 g/1 oz self-raising flour**
☐ **2 eggs**
☐ **200 g/6^1/$_2$ oz milk chocolate, melted and cooled**
☐ **185 g/6 oz chocolate chips**

1 Place butter and sugar in a food processor and process until mixture is creamy. Add flour and self-raising flour, eggs and melted chocolate and process until smooth. Stir in chocolate chips.
2 Place spoonfuls of mixture on greased baking trays and bake for 8-10 minutes or until just firm. Stand on trays for 5 minutes before transferring to wire racks to cool completely.

Double-Choc Cookies, Quick Nut Fudge Cake

7

A chocolate roll filled with chocolate cream makes a special afternoon tea treat or dessert. Irresistibly good to eat, these spectacular cakes are easy to make. Follow these step-by-step instructions for a perfect result every time.

CHOCOLATE ROLL

Serves 8
Oven temperature 180°C, 350°F, Gas 4

- [ ] **5 eggs, separated**
- [ ] **$^1/_4$ cup/60 g/2 oz caster sugar**
- [ ] **100 g/3$^1/_2$ oz dark chocolate, melted and cooled**
- [ ] **2 tablespoons self-raising flour, sifted with 2 tablespoons cocoa powder**

CHOCOLATE FILLING
- [ ] **60 g/2 oz dark chocolate**
- [ ] **$^2/_3$ cup/170 mL/5$^1/_2$ fl oz cream (double)**

1 Place egg yolks and sugar in a mixing bowl and beat until mixture is thick and creamy. Beat in chocolate, then fold in flour mixture.

2 Beat egg whites until stiff peaks form and fold into chocolate mixture. Pour into a greased and lined 26 x 32 cm/10$^1/_2$ x 12$^3/_4$ in Swiss roll tin and bake for 12-15 minutes or until just firm. Turn onto a damp teatowel sprinkled with caster sugar and roll up from the short end. Set aside to cool.

3 To make filling, place chocolate and cream in a small saucepan and cook over a low heat until chocolate melts and mixture is well blended. Bring to the boil, remove from heat and set aside to cool, completely. When cold, place in a mixing bowl over ice and beat until thick and creamy.

4 Unroll cake, spread with filling and reroll. To serve, cut into slices.

Beat egg whites until stiff peaks form and fold into chocolate mixture.

Turn cake onto a damp teatowel sprinkled with caster sugar and roll up from the short end.

Unroll cake, spread with filling and reroll.

9

Plates Villeroy & Boch

CHOCOLATE CHERRY STRUDEL

Layers of filo pastry and grated chocolate wrapped around a cherry filling make a wonderful combination.

Serves 10
Oven temperature 220°C, 425°F, Gas 7

- ☐ **8 sheets filo pastry**
- ☐ **15 g/¹/2 oz butter, melted**
- ☐ **100 g/3¹/2 oz dark chocolate, grated**

CHERRY FILLING
- ☐ **¹/2 cup/125 g/4 oz sour cream**
- ☐ **2 teaspoons brandy**
- ☐ **1 tablespoon raw (muscovado) sugar**
- ☐ **440 g/14 oz canned pitted black cherries, drained**

1   To make filling, place sour cream, brandy and sugar in a mixing bowl and beat until smooth and well combined. Stir in cherries.
2   Layer sheets of pastry, brushing every second sheet with butter and sprinkling with chocolate. Finish with a layer of chocolate.

3   Spoon filling down centre of pastry. Fold in short ends, then starting from long end roll up. Place strudel on a well-greased baking tray, brush with remaining butter and bake for 10 minutes. Reduce oven temperature to 180°C/350°F/Gas 4 and bake for 20-30 minutes longer or until golden brown. Serve warm with whipped cream if desired.
Cook's tip: An easy way to grate chocolate is to use the food processor with the shredding disc. Place the chocolate in the feed tube and press down firmly on the chocolate.

CHOCOLATE COFFEE TUILES

Tiny mocha-flavoured tuiles that are wonderful to serve after dinner with coffee.

Makes 25
Oven temperature 180°C, 350°F, Gas 4

- ☐ **2 egg whites**
- ☐ **¹/2 cup/100 g/3¹/2 oz caster sugar**
- ☐ **¹/2 teaspoon instant coffee powder dissolved in ¹/2 teaspoon water**

Chocolate Cherry Strudel, Chocolate Coffee Tuiles

- ☐ **1 teaspoon vanilla essence**
- ☐ **3 teaspoons cocoa powder**
- ☐ **4 teaspoons milk**
- ☐ **60 g/2 oz butter, melted and cooled**

1   Beat egg whites until soft peaks form. Gradually add sugar, beating well after each addition, until mixture is glossy and sugar dissolved. Fold in coffee mixture, vanilla essence, cocoa powder, milk and butter.
2   Drop spoonfuls of mixture 10 cm/4 in apart onto a greased baking tray and bake for 5 minutes or until edges are set. Remove from tray and wrap each biscuit around the handle of a wooden spoon. Allow to cool for 2 minutes, or until set, and set aside. Repeat with remaining mixture.
Cook's tip: Cook only one tray of tuiles at a time and work quickly when moulding, as they set very quickly. If the tuiles set before being moulded, return them to the oven for 30 seconds to 1 minute so that they regain their pliability.

CHOCOLATE SANDWICH CAKE

Makes a 20 cm/8 in sandwich cake
Oven temperature 180°C, 350°F, Gas 4

- ☐ **1 cup/125 g/4 oz self-raising flour, sifted**
- ☐ **¹/₄ teaspoon bicarbonate of soda**
- ☐ **¹/₂ cup/45 g/1¹/₂ oz cocoa powder, sifted**
- ☐ **125 g/4 oz butter, softened**
- ☐ **³/₄ cup/170 g/5¹/₂ oz caster sugar**
- ☐ **2 eggs, lightly beaten**
- ☐ **1 cup/250 g/8 oz sour cream**
- ☐ **¹/₂ cup/125 mL/4 fl oz cream (double), whipped**

CHOCOLATE ICING
- ☐ **60 g/2 oz dark chocolate, chopped**
- ☐ **30 g/1 oz unsalted butter**

1   Place flour, bicarbonate of soda, cocoa powder, butter, sugar, eggs and sour cream in a large mixing bowl and beat until well combined and mixture is smooth.

2   Spoon batter into two greased and lined 20 cm/8 in sandwich tins and bake for 25-30 minutes or until cooked when tested with a skewer. Stand cakes in tins for 5 minutes before turning onto a wire rack to cool.

3   Sandwich cold cakes together with whipped cream.

4   To make icing, place chocolate and butter in a small saucepan and cook over a low heat, stirring constantly, until melted. Cool slightly then spread over top of cake.

CHOCOLATE PINWHEELS

Layers of plain and chocolate dough are rolled together to make these delicious biscuits.

Makes 30
Oven temperature 180°C, 350°F, Gas 4

- ☐ **125 g/4 oz butter**
- ☐ **²/₃ cup/140g/4¹/₂ oz caster sugar**
- ☐ **1 teaspoon vanilla essence**
- ☐ **1 egg**
- ☐ **1³/₄ cups/220 g/7 oz flour, sifted**
- ☐ **¹/₄ cup/30 g/1 oz cocoa powder, sifted**

1   Place butter, sugar and vanilla essence in a mixing bowl and beat until mixture is creamy. Add egg and beat until well combined.

2   Divide mixture into two equal portions and mix 1 cup/125 g/4 oz flour into one portion and remaining flour and cocoa powder into the other portion.

3   Roll out each portion between two sheets of greaseproof paper to form a 20 x 30 cm/8 x 12 in rectangle. Remove top sheet of paper from each and invert one onto the other. Roll up from longer edge to form a long roll. Wrap in plastic food wrap and refrigerate for 1 hour.

4   Cut roll into 5 mm/¹/₄ in slices and place on greased baking trays. Bake for 10-12 minutes or until lightly browned. Cool on wire racks.

Cook's tip: These are ideal last-minute biscuits. The dough can be made in advance and kept in the refrigerator until needed.

*Chocolate Sandwich Cake,
Chocolate Pinwheels*

Tiles Fred Pazotti Marble board and rolling pin Butler & Co. Plate Waterford Wedgwood

12

COCONUT

The fruit of a tropical palm tree, coconut is mostly used in its desiccated or shredded form for baking. It adds a distinctive flavour and a moistness to baked goods that usually means they keep well. Toasted or left plain it is a wonderfully easy decoration.

Left: Coconut Cake, Oaty Choc-Chip Biscuits, Orange Coconut Loaf (all recipes page 14)

COCONUT CAKE

This light moist sponge-type cake, covered with a white frosting and topped with shredded coconut is a must for any afternoon tea.

Makes a 23 cm/9 in round cake
Oven temperature 180°C, 350°F, Gas 4

- ☐ 125 g/4 oz butter, softened
- ☐ 1 teaspoon vanilla essence
- ☐ 1 cup/220 g/7 oz caster sugar
- ☐ 3 egg whites
- ☐ 2 cups/250 g/8 oz self-raising flour, sifted
- ☐ ³/₄ cup/185 mL/6 fl oz milk
- ☐ 90 g/3 oz shredded coconut

FLUFFY FROSTING
- ☐ ¹/₂ cup/125 mL/4 fl oz water
- ☐ 1¹/₄ cups/315 g/10 oz sugar
- ☐ 3 egg whites
- ☐ 1 teaspoon lemon juice

1 Place butter and vanilla essence in a mixing bowl and beat until light and fluffy. Gradually add caster sugar, beating well after each addition until mixture is creamy.
2 Beat in egg whites, one at a time. Fold flour and milk, alternately, into creamed mixture. Divide batter evenly between two greased and lined 23 cm/9 in sandwich tins and bake for 25-30 minutes or until cakes are cooked when tested with a skewer. Stand in tins for 5 minutes before turning onto a wire rack to cool.
3 To make frosting, place water and sugar in a saucepan and cook over a medium heat, without boiling, stirring constantly until sugar dissolves. Brush any sugar from sides of pan using a pastry brush dipped in water. Bring syrup to the boil and boil rapidly for 3-5 minutes, without stirring, or until syrup reaches the soft ball stage (115°C/239°F on a sweet thermometer). Place egg whites in a mixing bowl and beat until soft peaks form. Continue beating while pouring in syrup in a thin stream a little at a time. Continue beating until all syrup is used and frosting will stand in stiff peaks. Beat in lemon juice.
4 Spread one cake with a little frosting and sprinkle with 2 tablespoons coconut, then top with remaining cake. Spread remaining frosting over top and sides of cake and sprinkle with remaining coconut.
Cook's tip: This cake looks pretty when decorated with edible flowers such as violets, rose petals or borage.

OATY CHOC-CHIP BISCUITS

A large biscuit that is ideal for lunch boxes or as an after-school or after-work treat.

Makes 25
Oven temperature 190°C, 375°F, Gas 5

- ☐ 125 g/4 oz butter, softened
- ☐ ¹/₂ teaspoon vanilla essence
- ☐ ³/₄ cup/125 g/4 oz soft brown sugar
- ☐ 1 egg
- ☐ ¹/₂ teaspoon bicarbonate of soda dissolved in 4 teaspoons warm water
- ☐ ³/₄ cup/90 g/3 oz flour, sifted
- ☐ 1¹/₂ cups/140 g/4¹/₂ oz rolled oats
- ☐ 45 g/1¹/₂ oz desiccated coconut
- ☐ 185 g/6 oz chocolate chips
- ☐ 75 g/2¹/₂ oz raisins

1 Place butter, vanilla essence and sugar in a mixing bowl and beat until light and creamy. Beat in egg, bicarbonate of soda mixture and flour.
2 Stir in oats, coconut, chocolate chips and raisins. Place rounded tablespoons of mixture 10 cm/4 in apart on greased baking trays. Using a knife, spread out each mound of mixture to form a thin round, 7.5 cm/3 in in diameter. Bake for 8-10 minutes or until golden. Transfer to wire racks to cool.

ORANGE COCONUT LOAF

Makes an 11 x 21 cm/4¹/₂ x 8¹/₂ in loaf
Oven temperature 180°C, 350°F, Gas 4

- ☐ 1 cup/220 g/7 oz caster sugar
- ☐ 90 g/3 oz butter, softened
- ☐ 1 teaspoon vanilla essence
- ☐ 3 teaspoons finely grated orange rind
- ☐ ³/₄ cup/185 mL/6 fl oz coconut milk
- ☐ 3 egg whites
- ☐ 1²/₃ cups/200 g/6¹/₂ oz self-raising flour, sifted
- ☐ 1 teaspoon baking powder

1 Place sugar, butter, vanilla essence and orange rind in a food processor and process until combined. Add coconut milk, egg whites, flour and baking powder and process until just combined and smooth.
2 Pour batter into a greased and lined 11 x 21 cm/4¹/₂ x 8¹/₂ in loaf tin and bake for 35-40 minutes or until cooked when tested with a skewer. Stand for 5 minutes in tin before turning onto a wire rack to cool.

LIME AND COCONUT COOKIES

The tang of lime and the unique flavour and texture of coconut combine to make these wonderful cookies.

Makes 35
Oven temperature 180°C, 350°F, Gas 4

- ☐ 125 g/4 oz butter, chopped
- ☐ 1 cup/170 g/5¹/₂ oz soft brown sugar
- ☐ 1 teaspoon vanilla essence
- ☐ 1 egg
- ☐ 1 cup/125 g/4 oz flour
- ☐ ¹/₂ cup/60 g/2 oz self-raising flour
- ☐ 1 cup/90 g/3 oz rolled oats
- ☐ 45 g/1¹/₂ oz desiccated coconut
- ☐ 2 teaspoons finely grated lime rind
- ☐ 2 tablespoons lime juice

1 Place butter, sugar, vanilla essence, egg, flour and self-raising flour, rolled oats, coconut, lime rind and lime juice in a food processor and process until well combined.
2 Place heaped spoonfuls of mixture on greased baking trays and bake for 12-15 minutes or until lightly browned. Cool on wire racks.

GOLDEN OAT BISCUITS

Golden, crunchy and delicious, these biscuits won't last long.

Makes 30
Oven temperature 180°C, 350°F, Gas 4

- ☐ 1 cup/90 g/3 oz rolled oats
- ☐ 1 cup/125 g/4 oz flour, sifted
- ☐ 90 g/3 oz desiccated coconut
- ☐ 1 cup/250 g/8 oz sugar
- ☐ 4 teaspoons golden syrup, warmed
- ☐ 125 g/4 oz butter, melted
- ☐ 2 tablespoons boiling water
- ☐ 1 teaspoon bicarbonate of soda

1 Place oats, flour, coconut and sugar in a large mixing bowl. Combine golden syrup, butter, water and bicarbonate of soda.
2 Pour golden syrup mixture into dry ingredients and mix well to combine. Place spoonfuls of mixture 3 cm/1¹/₄ in apart on greased baking trays and bake for 10-15 minutes or until biscuits are just firm. Stand on trays for 3 minutes before transferring to wire racks to cool.

Golden Oat Biscuits,
Lime and Coconut Cookies

PROCESSOR MAGIC

Your food processor or hand blender will quickly chop the fruit and nuts for this delectable slice. There's no fuss and only one bowl.

PROCESSOR KNOW-HOW

The following is a general guide to using your food processor, however it is important to read the manufacturer's handbook so that you can make full use of your machine and be aware of the safety and care features.

Chopping: To chop ingredients, use the metal chopping blade. First cut solid ingredients, such as butter and fresh fruit, into large pieces, then place in the processor bowl and chop roughly, using the pulse button. For finely chopped ingredients, pulse several times.

To grind ingredients such as nuts, process for a short time, taking care not to make a paste.

Shredding: To shred ingredients, use the shredding disc. Place food in the feed tube and, with the machine running, exert a small amount of pressure on the food. This attachment is ideal for shredding carrots for carrot cake and by using a little more pressure, it is a good way to

grate a quantity of chocolate.

Mixing: To mix ingredients, use the metal chopping blade. To cream butter and sugar, roughly chop the butter and place with the sugar in the processor bowl, then process until mixture is light and creamy. If necessary, scrape down the sides of the bowl several times during processing. Add eggs and process to mix, then add dry ingredients.

Crumbing biscuits: To make biscuit crumbs, use the metal chopping blade. Place biscuits in the processor bowl and process until biscuits are crumbed.

CHOCOLATE FRUIT AND NUT BARS

Use your food processor to prepare and mix these bars in minutes.

Makes 25
Oven temperature 180°C, 350°F, Gas 4

- ☐ **155 g/5 oz almonds, chopped**
- ☐ **125 g hazelnuts, chopped**
- ☐ **125 g/4 oz dried apricots, chopped**
- ☐ **125 g/4 oz glacé cherries, chopped**
- ☐ **90 g/3 oz desiccated coconut**
- ☐ **1/4 cup/60 g/2 oz caster sugar**
- ☐ **1/4 cup/30 g/1 oz flour**
- ☐ **250 g/8 oz dark chocolate, melted**
- ☐ **1/4 cup/75 g/2 1/2 oz apricot jam**
- ☐ **icing sugar**

1 Place almonds, hazelnuts, apricots, cherries, coconut, sugar and flour in a food processor and process to combine. With machine running, add chocolate and jam and process until ingredients are combined.

2 Press mixture into a greased and lined shallow 18 x 28 cm/7 x 11 in cake tin and bake for 25-30 minutes or until firm. Set aside to cool in tin. Dust with icing sugar and cut into bars.

WHICH FOOD PROCESSOR?

There are two types of food processors – the one that stands on the bench and the hand blender. Both play an important role in food preparation and are useful for slicing, chopping, grinding and mixing.

The Hand Held Blender: This relatively new appliance is ideal for chopping, mincing and grinding small quantities of food. Everything from meat to nuts can be processed using this handy appliance. The hand held blender comes with its own chopping bowl and beaker. It can be used with these accessories or in an ordinary mixing bowl. When baking, use the hand blender for chopping nuts, puréeing fruit, grating hard cheese and chocolate, mixing batters for pancakes and crêpes, and chopping dried fruit. It is a light, easily managed appliance, particularly suited to disabled and arthritic cooks, as those difficult and fiddly jobs of cutting and chopping are quickly and safely achieved. Children can easily and safely make milkshakes using the hand held blender. It is also great for puréeing soups as the blender can be taken to the bowl or saucepan.

The Food Processor: This appliance is ideal for larger quantities of food. Cakes, biscuits and slices are mixed in seconds and pastry is made in minutes. Take the hard work out of making homemade bread and use the dough hook for kneading. The food processor will chop, grind, mince and purée. Throughout this book you will find many recipes made in the food processor showing just how versatile this appliance is for baking.

For many recipes, the food processor can take the place of an electric mixer when creaming butter and sugar, mixing cake batters and making one bowl biscuits and slices. If processing a number of ingredients, which are to be combined for the same recipe, it is not necessary to wash the processor bowl between each ingredient. However, you should arrange your processing so that the dry ingredients are processed first. Once the individual ingredients are prepared, you can then return all the ingredients to the food processor for final mixing and in this way save on washing up by using only one bowl.

FRUIT AND NUTS

F*ruit and nuts are healthy additions to any baked product and add flavour, crunch and texture. It's usually safe to substitute your favourite fruit or nuts in a recipe and still end up with a delicious cake, biscuit or slice.*

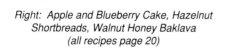

Right: Apple and Blueberry Cake, Hazelnut Shortbreads, Walnut Honey Baklava (all recipes page 20)

APPLE AND BLUEBERRY CAKE

Makes a 20 cm/8 in round cake
Oven temperature 180°C, 350°F, Gas 4

- ☐ **125 g/4oz butter, softened**
- ☐ **1 teaspoon vanilla essence**
- ☐ **3/4 cup/170 g/5¹/2 oz caster sugar**
- ☐ **2 eggs, lightly beaten**
- ☐ **1¹/2 cups/185 g/6 oz self-raising flour, sifted**
- ☐ **1/2 cup/125 mL/4 fl oz buttermilk or milk**
- ☐ **220 g/7 oz canned apple slices**
- ☐ **220 g/7 oz canned blueberries, well drained**

CINNAMON TOPPING
- ☐ **4 teaspoons caster sugar**
- ☐ **1 teaspoon ground cinnamon**

1 Place butter, vanilla essence, sugar, eggs, flour and milk in a mixing bowl and beat well until ingredients are combined and mixture is smooth.
2 Spoon half the batter into a greased and lined 20 cm/8 in round cake tin. Top with half the apple slices and half the blueberries, then remaining batter. Arrange remaining apple and blueberries over top of batter.
3 To make topping, combine sugar and cinnamon and sprinkle over cake. Bake for 55-60 minutes or until cake is cooked when tested with a skewer. Stand in tin for 10 minutes before turning onto a wire rack to cool.
Variation: You may like to try replacing the blueberries in this recipe with canned blackberries.

FLORENTINE SQUARES

An easy version of florentines you are sure to want to make time and again.

Makes 30
Oven temperature 160°C, 325°F, Gas 3

- ☐ **125 g/4 oz raisins, finely chopped**
- ☐ **2 cups/90 g/3 oz corn flakes, crushed**
- ☐ **90 g/3 oz slivered almonds, toasted**
- ☐ **90 g/3 oz glacé cherries, chopped**
- ☐ **2/3 cup/170 mL/5¹/2 fl oz sweetened condensed milk**
- ☐ **100 g/3¹/2 oz dark chocolate, melted**

1 Place raisins, corn flakes, almonds, cherries and condensed milk in a large mixing bowl and mix well to combine.

SUGAR SUBSTITUTES

If the recipe calls for:	You can use:
Caster sugar	Superfine sugar, or place granulated sugar in a food processor or blender and process to make finer.
Demerara or muscovado sugar	Raw sugar
Icing sugar	Confectioners' sugar

2 Spoon mixture into a greased and lined 23 cm/9 in square cake tin. Press down firmly using a fork and bake for 25-30 minutes or until firm. Stand in tin for 5 minutes before turning onto a wire rack to cool.
3 Cut into squares, then dip one corner of each square in melted chocolate. Set aside on a sheet of aluminium foil until chocolate sets.

HAZELNUT SHORTBREADS

Ground hazelnuts give a deliciously different shortbread.

Makes 40
Oven temperature 160°C, 325°F, Gas 3

- ☐ **1¹/2 cups/185 g/6 oz flour, sifted**
- ☐ **45 g/1¹/2 oz hazelnuts, ground**
- ☐ **1/4 cup/45 g/1¹/2 oz ground rice**
- ☐ **250 g/8 oz butter, cut into small pieces**
- ☐ **1/4 cup/60 g/2 oz caster sugar**
- ☐ **100 g/3¹/2 oz chocolate, melted**

1 Place flour, hazelnuts and ground rice in a food processor, add butter and process until mixture resembles coarse bread crumbs. Add sugar and process to combine.
2 Turn mixture onto a floured surface and knead lightly to make a pliable dough. Place dough between sheets of baking paper and roll out to 5 mm/¹/4 in thick. Using a 5 cm/2 in fluted pastry cutter, cut out rounds of dough and place 3 cm/1 in apart on greased baking trays. Bake for 20-25 minutes or until lightly browned. Stand on baking trays for 2-3 minutes before transferring to wire racks to cool completely.
3 Place melted chocolate in a plastic food bag, snip off one corner and pipe lines across each biscuit.

WALNUT HONEY BAKLAVA

The secret to this Middle Eastern specialty is to pour the hot syrup over the hot pastry.

Makes 20
Oven temperature 220°C, 425°F, Gas 7

- ☐ **375 g/12 oz filo pastry**
- ☐ **155 g/5 oz butter, melted**

WALNUT FILLING
- ☐ **250 g/8 oz finely chopped walnuts, toasted**
- ☐ **1 teaspoon ground cinnamon**
- ☐ **1 teaspoon ground mixed spice**
- ☐ **1/3 cup/60 g/2 oz soft brown sugar**

HONEY ORANGE SYRUP
- ☐ **1/2 cup/125 mL/4 fl oz water**
- ☐ **1/3 cup/90 g/3 oz sugar**
- ☐ **1/3 cup/125 g/4 oz honey**
- ☐ **1/3 cup/90 mL/3 fl oz freshly squeezed orange juice**
- ☐ **2 tablespoons lemon juice**

1 To make filling, combine walnuts, cinnamon, mixed spice and brown sugar in a bowl and set aside.
2 Cut pastry sheets into 18 x 28 cm/7 x 11 in rectangles. Layer a quarter of the pastry sheets in a greased, shallow 18 x 28 cm/7 x 11 in cake tin, brushing each sheet with butter. Sprinkle pastry with one-third of filling, repeat with remaining pastry and filling, finish with a layer of pastry.
3 Cut pastry into squares using a sharp knife. Brush top with butter and bake for 15 minutes. Reduce oven temperature to 190°C/375°F/Gas 5 and bake for 10 minutes longer or until golden brown.
4 To make syrup, place water, sugar, honey, orange juice and lemon juice in a small saucepan and cook over a medium heat, stirring constantly, until sugar dissolves. Bring to the boil, then remove from heat and pour over hot baklava. Set aside and allow to cool completely in tin.

MINI APRICOT TURNOVERS

*Tiny turnovers are delicious eaten hot,
warm or cold with whipped cream
and make a great dessert for
casual entertaining.*

Makes 16
Oven temperature 220°C, 425°F, Gas 7

- ☐ **750 g/1¹/₂ lb prepared or ready-rolled puff pastry**
- ☐ **1 tablespoon water**
- ☐ **1 tablespoon milk**
- ☐ **1 tablespoon demerara sugar**

APRICOT FILLING
- ☐ **440 g/14 oz canned apricots, drained and sliced**
- ☐ **60 g/2 oz chopped hazelnuts, toasted**
- ☐ **45 g/1¹/₂ oz glacé ginger, chopped**
- ☐ **2 tablespoons soft brown sugar**
- ☐ **1 teaspoon ground mixed spice**

1 To make filling, place apricots, hazelnuts, ginger, brown sugar and mixed spice in a bowl and mix to combine.

2 Roll out pastry to 3 mm/¹/₈ in thick and cut out sixteen rounds using a 10 cm/ 4 in pastry cutter. Place a spoonful of filling in the centre of each pastry round. Brush edges with a little water, fold pastry over to form a half circle and press together using a fork to seal and make a decorative edge. Brush each turnover with milk and sprinkle with a little demerara sugar. Place on wet baking trays and bake for 12-15 minutes or until puffed and golden.

Variation: You might like to try making these with canned peaches or apples instead of apricots.

Florentine Squares, Mini Apricot Turnovers

NUT MILLE FEUILLES

These delicious pastry stacks filled with a coconut and nut filling are a quick dessert idea. Macadamia nuts or brazil nuts can be used in the nut filling.

Serves 6
Oven temperature 200°C, 400°F, Gas 6

- [ ] **200 g/6$^{1}/_{2}$ oz prepared or ready-rolled puff pastry**
- [ ] **icing sugar**

COCONUT FILLING
- [ ] **2 egg yolks**
- [ ] **2 tablespoons caster sugar**
- [ ] **4 teaspoons cornflour**
- [ ] **$^{1}/_{2}$ teaspoon vanilla essence**
- [ ] **$^{1}/_{2}$ cup/125 mL/4 fl oz cream (double)**
- [ ] **$^{1}/_{2}$ cup/125 mL/4 fl oz coconut milk**
- [ ] **30 g/1 oz desiccated coconut**

NUT FILLING
- [ ] **45 g/1$^{1}/_{2}$ oz unsalted macadamia or brazil nuts, finely chopped**
- [ ] **2 tablespoons sour cream**
- [ ] **1$^{1}/_{2}$ tablespoons soft brown sugar**
- [ ] **2 teaspoons dark rum**

1   Roll out pastry to 3 mm/$^{1}/_{8}$ in thick and cut out nine rounds using a 7.5 cm/3 in pastry cutter. Place on a greased baking tray and bake for 10 minutes or until puffed and golden brown. Cool on a wire rack.
2   To make Coconut Filling, place egg yolks, sugar, cornflour and vanilla essence in a mixing bowl and beat to combine. Place cream and coconut milk in a saucepan and bring just to the boil. Remove from heat and gradually whisk into egg mixture. Return mixture to pan and cook over a low heat, stirring constantly, until mixture thickens and coats the back of a wooden spoon. Stir in coconut. Cover surface of custard with plastic food wrap and set aside to cool.
3   To make Nut Filling, place nuts, sour cream, sugar and rum in a mixing bowl and mix until well combined. Set aside.
4   To assemble mille feuilles, split each pastry round into two layers. Spread a round with Coconut Filling, top with another pastry layer, then spread with Nut Filling and finish with a final layer of pastry. Repeat with remaining pastry layers and fillings. To serve, dust with icing sugar.
Cook's tip: If unsalted macadamia nuts are unavailable you can use salted macadamia nuts that have been rinsed under cold running water then dried in the oven for 10 minutes at 150°C/300°F/ Gas 2. Take care not to toast the nuts.

CHERRY AND APPLE FLAN

Makes a 10 x 33 cm/4 x 13$^{1}/_{4}$ in flan
Oven temperature 200°C, 400°F, Gas 6

- [ ] **300 g/9$^{1}/_{2}$ oz prepared or ready-rolled shortcrust pastry**

CHERRY FILLING
- [ ] **30 g/1 oz butter**
- [ ] **2 apples, cored, peeled and sliced**
- [ ] **440 g/14 oz bottled pitted morello cherries, drained**
- [ ] **1 teaspoon ground cinnamon**
- [ ] **2 eggs, lightly beaten**
- [ ] **$^{1}/_{2}$ cup/125 mL/4 fl oz cream (double)**
- [ ] **$^{1}/_{3}$ cup/60 g/2 oz soft brown sugar**
- [ ] **4 teaspoons flour**
- [ ] **1 teaspoon vanilla essence**

1   Roll out pastry to 3 mm/$^{1}/_{8}$ in thick and line a greased 10 x 33 cm/4 x 13$^{1}/_{4}$ in flan tin. Line pastry case with nonstick baking paper, fill with uncooked rice and bake blind for 10 minutes. Remove rice and paper and bake for 10 minutes longer. Set aside to cool.
2   To make filling, melt butter in a frying pan and cook apples for 3-4 minutes. Remove from heat and set aside to cool.
3   Arrange apples and cherries over base of pastry case and sprinkle with cinnamon. Combine eggs, cream, sugar, flour and vanilla essence and beat until smooth. Pour over fruit in pastry case. Reduce oven temperature to 190°C/375°F/Gas 5 and bake for 30-35 minutes or until filling is set. Serve warm.

China Villeroy & Boch

Cherry and Apple Flan, Nut Mille Feuilles

sweet NOTES

The earliest sweeteners were honey, sweet fruits and syrups extracted from fruit. These are still used but by far the most popular sweetener today is white table sugar.

&- In baking, sugar acts not only as a sweetener, but also helps to produce a soft, spongy texture and improves the keeping quality of cakes.

&- Caster sugar is the best white sugar for making most cakes as it dissolves quickly and easily.

&- Granulated sugar is coarser than caster sugar and although it is often used in cake making it can result in a cake with a slightly reduced volume and a speckled crust.

&- Brown sugar can be used in place of caster sugar, however it gives a richer flavour and colour to the cake.

&- Icing sugar is not usually used in cake making, as it gives a cake of poor volume and a hard crust. It is, however, ideal for icings.

&- In cakes that use the melt-and-mix method – the melted fat and sugar mixture is added to the dry ingredients – granulated, raw or demerara sugars can be used, as the sugar is dissolved before baking.

&- Honey adds a distinctive flavour to baked products and makes them dense and moist with better keeping qualities.

&- If using honey in place of sugar, reduce the amount of honey used by one-quarter and bake at a slightly lower temperature. Baked products made with honey brown more quickly than those made with sugar.

Finding an ingredient hidden inside a loaf of bread or a cake is always fun. To make sure the berries stay hidden in this Easy Berry Bread during cooking do not overfill the bread. Follow these easy step-by-step instructions and make this Easy Berry Bread.

EASY BERRY BREAD

Makes an 18 cm/7 in round
Oven temperature 220°C, 425°F, Gas 7

- ☐ **3 cups/375 g/12 oz self-raising flour**
- ☐ **1 teaspoon baking powder**
- ☐ **1^1/2 teaspoons ground mixed spice**
- ☐ **1^1/2 tablespoons sugar**
- ☐ **30 g/1 oz butter**
- ☐ **^{1}/2 cup/125 mL/4 fl oz milk**
- ☐ **^{2}/3 cup/170 mL/5^1/2 fl oz water**
- ☐ **200 g/6^1/2 oz raspberries**
- ☐ **1 tablespoon caster sugar**
- ☐ **4 teaspoons milk**

Make a well in the centre of flour mixture and, using a round-ended knife, mix in milk and water to form a soft dough.

1 Sift together flour, baking powder and mixed spice into a mixing bowl. Add sugar and rub in butter using fingertips until mixture resembles coarse bread crumbs.
2 Make a well in the centre of flour mixture and, using a round-ended knife, mix in milk and water. Mix to form a soft dough.
3 Turn dough onto a floured surface and knead lightly until smooth. Divide dough into two portions and flatten each into an 18 cm/7 in round. Sprinkle raspberries and sugar over surface of one round leaving 2.5 cm/1 in around edge. Brush edge with a little milk and place remaining round on top. Seal edges securely using fingertips.
4 Place on a greased and lightly floured baking tray. Brush surface with milk and bake for 10 minutes. Reduce oven temperature to 180°C/350°F/Gas 4 and bake for 20-25 minutes longer or until cooked through.

Divide dough into two portions and flatten each into an 18 cm/7 in round. Sprinkle raspberries and sugar over one round leaving 2.5 cm/1 in around edge.

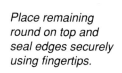

Place remaining round on top and seal edges securely using fingertips.

26

ORANGES
AND LEMONS

As an ingredient or decoration, the freshly grated zest of oranges, lemons or limes adds a distinctive taste to any cookie, biscuit or slice. Aromatic citrus fruits have found their way into every aspect of cooking – sweet and savoury. Using these delicious recipes fill your tins and jars with unforgettable goodies.

Left: Choc-Chip and Orange Cake, Lemon Marshmallow Slice, Orange Pecan Loaf (all recipes page 28)

LEMON AND LIME BARS

Makes 30
Oven temperature 190°C, 375°F, Gas 5

- ☐ **125 g/4 oz butter**
- ☐ **1 cup/125 g/4 oz flour**
- ☐ **$^1/_2$ cup/75 g/2$^1/_2$ oz icing sugar**
- ☐ **icing sugar, to dust**

LEMON AND LIME TOPPING
- ☐ **2 eggs, lightly beaten**
- ☐ **1 cup/220 g/7 oz caster sugar**
- ☐ **4 teaspoons flour**
- ☐ **4 teaspoons lemon juice**
- ☐ **2 tablespoons lime juice**
- ☐ **1 teaspoon finely grated lemon rind**

1   Place butter, flour and icing sugar in a food processor and process to form a soft dough. Turn dough onto a lightly floured surface and knead lightly. Press dough into a greased and lined shallow 18 x 28 cm/7 x 11 in cake tin and bake for 20 minutes or until firm. Allow to cool in tin.
2   To make topping, place eggs, sugar, flour, lemon juice, lime juice and lemon rind in a mixing bowl and mix until combined. Pour over cooked base and cook for 25-30 minutes longer or until firm. Refrigerate until cold, then cut into bars. Just prior to serving, dust with icing sugar.

CHOC-CHIP AND ORANGE CAKE

Makes a 20 cm/8 in ring cake
Oven temperature 180°C, 350°F, Gas 4

- ☐ **125 g/4 oz butter, softened**
- ☐ **2 teaspoons grated orange rind**
- ☐ **$^3/_4$ cup/170 g/5$^1/_2$ oz caster sugar**
- ☐ **2 eggs, lightly beaten**
- ☐ **1$^1/_2$ cups/185 g/6 oz self-raising flour, sifted**
- ☐ **2 tablespoons freshly squeezed orange juice**
- ☐ **$^1/_2$ cup/100 g/3$^1/_2$ oz natural yogurt**
- ☐ **$^1/_4$ cup/60 mL/2 fl oz milk**
- ☐ **100 g/3$^1/_2$ oz roughly grated chocolate**

CHOCOLATE ICING
- ☐ **45 g/1$^1/_2$ oz butter, softened**
- ☐ **$^1/_2$ teaspoon grated orange rind**
- ☐ **$^3/_4$ cup/125 g/4 oz icing sugar, sifted**
- ☐ **1$^1/_2$ tablespoons cocoa powder, sifted**
- ☐ **4 teaspoons freshly squeezed orange juice**

1   Place butter, orange rind, sugar, eggs, flour, orange juice, yogurt and milk in a large mixing bowl and beat until all ingredients are combined and batter is smooth. Fold in grated chocolate.
2   Spoon batter into a greased 20 cm/8 in ring cake tin and bake for 45-50 minutes or until cake is cooked when tested with a skewer. Stand cake in tin for 5 minutes before turning onto a wire rack to cool.
3   To make icing, place butter and orange rind in a mixing bowl and beat until creamy. Add icing sugar, cocoa and orange juice and beat until combined. Add a little more orange juice if necessary. Place in a heatproof bowl over a saucepan of simmering water and cook, stirring constantly, for 2-3 minutes or until mixture is smooth and runny. Pour icing over cold cake.

ORANGE PECAN LOAF

This orange-flavoured carrot loaf spiced with cardamom and studded with pecans is a far cry from the carrot cake of days past.

Makes an 11 x 21 cm /4$^1/_2$ x 8$^1/_2$ in loaf
Oven temperature 180°C, 350°F, Gas 4

- ☐ **$^1/_2$ cup/60 g/2 oz flour**
- ☐ **1 cup/125 g/4 oz self-raising flour**
- ☐ **$^1/_2$ teaspoon bicarbonate of soda**
- ☐ **$^1/_2$ teaspoon ground cardamom**
- ☐ **$^1/_2$ teaspoon ground nutmeg**
- ☐ **2 eggs**
- ☐ **1 cup/220 g/7 oz caster sugar**
- ☐ **$^1/_2$ cup/125 mL/4 fl oz vegetable oil**
- ☐ **$^1/_2$ teaspoon vanilla essence**
- ☐ **4 teaspoons freshly squeezed orange juice**
- ☐ **2 teaspoons finely grated orange rind**
- ☐ **100 g/3$^1/_2$ oz grated carrot**
- ☐ **60 g/2 oz pecans, chopped**

1   Sift together flour and self-raising flour, bicarbonate of soda, cardamom and nutmeg into a large bowl.
2   Place eggs and sugar in a mixing bowl and beat until creamy. Gradually add oil, beating well after each addition until mixture is thick and increased in volume. Mix in vanilla essence, orange juice and orange rind. Fold flour mixture into egg mixture, then mix in carrot and pecans.
3   Spoon mixture into a greased and lined 11 x 21 cm/4$^1/_2$ x 8$^1/_2$ in loaf tin and bake for 50 minutes or until cooked when tested with a skewer. Stand loaf in tin for 5 minutes before turning onto a wire rack to cool completely.

THE JUICIEST FRUIT

❧   If both the juice and rind of lemons, limes or oranges are to be used in a recipe, grate the rind first then squeeze the juice and pour over the rind. This will keep the rind fresh and moist while you are preparing the rest of the recipe.
❧   Warming citrus fruit in the oven or microwave oven also helps the fruit to yield more juice. When doing this, take care that you do not actually cook the fruit.
❧   To get the most juice from oranges, lemons or limes, have the fruit at room temperature, roll it between the palm of your hand and the work surface, then squeeze.
❧   Lemons and limes will keep in the refrigerator for up to four weeks.

LEMON MARSHMALLOW SLICE

A fluffy marshmallow topping combines with a crunchy coconut base to make this delicious no-bake slice.

Makes 30

- ☐ **100 g/3$^1/_2$ oz plain sweet biscuits, crushed**
- ☐ **60 g/2 oz butter, melted**
- ☐ **30 g/1 oz desiccated coconut**

LEMON MARSHMALLOW TOPPING
- ☐ **400 g/9$^1/_2$ oz white marshmallows**
- ☐ **4 teaspoons gelatine**
- ☐ **$^2/_3$ cup/170 mL/5$^1/_2$ fl oz milk**
- ☐ **$^1/_3$ cup/90 mL/3 fl oz lemon juice**
- ☐ **$^1/_2$ cup/90 g/3 oz finely grated lemon rind**

1   Place crushed biscuits, butter and coconut in a bowl and mix well to combine. Press mixture into a greased and lined shallow 18 x 28 cm/7 x 11 in cake tin. Refrigerate until firm.
2   To make filling, place marshmallows, gelatine, milk, lemon juice and rind in a saucepan and cook, stirring, over a low heat until mixture is smooth and gelatine dissolves. Remove from heat and allow to cool, stirring every 3-5 minutes. Pour over biscuit base and refrigerate until firm.
Lime Marshmallow Slice: Replace lemon juice and rind with lime juice and rind.

EASY LEMON AND ALMOND CAKE

Makes a 20 cm/8 in round cake
Oven temperature 180°C, 350°F, Gas 4

- ☐ **185 g/6 oz butter, softened**
- ☐ **¹/₂ cup/100 g/3¹/₂ oz caster sugar**
- ☐ **¹/₂ cup/185 g/4 oz prepared lemon butter (curd)**
- ☐ **3 eggs, lightly beaten**
- ☐ **1¹/₄ cups/155 g/5 oz self-raising flour, sifted**
- ☐ **30 g/1 oz ground almonds**
- ☐ **¹/₂ cup/125 mL/4 fl oz milk**
- ☐ **3 tablespoons flaked almonds, toasted**

LEMON FROSTING
- ☐ **125 g/4 oz cream cheese**
- ☐ **1 teaspoon finely grated lemon rind**
- ☐ **1¹/₂ cups/220 g/7 oz icing sugar**
- ☐ **2 teaspoons lemon juice**

1   Place butter, sugar, lemon butter, eggs, flour, ground almonds and milk in a large mixing bowl and beat well to combine all ingredients.

2   Spoon mixture into a greased and lined 20 cm/8 in round cake tin and bake for 40 minutes or until cooked when tested with a skewer. Stand cake in tin for 5 minutes before turning onto a wire rack to cool.

3   To make frosting, place cream cheese, lemon rind, icing sugar and lemon juice in a food processor and process for 1 minute or until frosting is of a spreadable consistency. Spread frosting over top of cold cake, then sprinkle with flaked almonds.

*Easy Lemon and Almond Cake,
Lemon and Lime Bars*

SOMETHING SAVOURY

Quick breads, true to their name, are quick – and easy – to bake. They use baking powder or bicarbonate of soda instead of yeast as the rising agent. In this chapter you will find wonderful recipes for quick breads and savoury pastry treats.

Right: Bacon Corn Bread Pots, Cheese Straws, Bacon and Leek Mini Quiches (all recipes page 32)

China Country Floors *Tiles* Fred Pazotti *Copper utensils* Accoutrement

THE BIG CHEESE

Cheese is a favourite ingredient for savoury baking. It adds a wonderful flavour and texture to baked goods whether sprinkled on the top or mixed into a mixture.

🐦 Cheese has a high fat content and like butter will absorb any strong flavours so should be kept tightly wrapped in aluminium foil or plastic food wrap.

🐦 Moisture can cause mould to form on the surface of cheese. Those cheeses that tend to mould quickly are best wrapped loosely in foil so the cheese can breathe and the moisture can escape.

🐦 Moulds that form on the surface of cheese are unattractive but not harmful. If mould has formed on your cheese you can just cut it away or scrape it off with a knife.

🐦 Hard cheese freezes well when grated and can be used straight from the freezer. To freeze cheese, simply place in a freezer bag and secure to make airtight.

🐦 As salt is added to cheese during processing many cheeses are quite salty, so go easy on salt in any recipe that has cheese in it.

BACON AND LEEK MINI QUICHES

Serve these tasty mini quiches hot, warm or cold.

Makes 20
Oven temperature 190°C, 375°F, Gas 5

- ☐ **750 g/1^1/2 lb prepared shortcrust pastry**

BACON AND LEEK FILLING
- ☐ **2 rashers bacon, finely chopped**
- ☐ **1 small leek, finely chopped**
- ☐ **1 tomato, finely chopped**
- ☐ **1 tablespoon finely chopped fresh basil**
- ☐ **freshly ground black pepper**
- ☐ **4 eggs, lightly beaten**
- ☐ **1^1/2 cups/375 mL/12 fl oz cream (single)**
- ☐ **60 g/2 oz grated tasty cheese (mature Cheddar)**

1 To make filling, cook bacon and leek in a nonstick frying pan, over a medium heat for 3-4 minutes, or until leek is soft. Remove from heat and stir in tomato, basil and black pepper to taste. Set aside to cool. Place eggs and cream in a bowl and whisk to combine.

2 Roll out pastry to 3 mm/^{1}/8 in thick and cut out twenty pastry rounds using a 10 cm/4 in pastry cutter and press lightly into greased flat-based patty pans (tartlet tins).

3 Place a little bacon mixture into each pastry case, spoon over egg mixture and sprinkle with cheese. Bake for 15-20 minutes or until filling is firm and pastry golden.

BACON CORN BREAD POTS

Cooked in flowerpots these tasty corn bread loaves are a perfect accompaniment to soup or salad.

Serves 6
Makes 3 medium flowerpot loaves
Oven temperature 200°C, 400°F, Gas 6

- ☐ **4 rashers bacon, finely chopped**
- ☐ **1^1/2 cups/250 g/8 oz fine corn meal (polenta)**
- ☐ **1 cup/125 g/4 oz flour**
- ☐ **2^1/2 teaspoons baking powder**
- ☐ **4 teaspoons sugar**
- ☐ **^{1}/2 teaspoon salt**
- ☐ **60 g/2 oz grated Parmesan cheese**
- ☐ **90 g/3 oz butter, chopped**
- ☐ **2 eggs, lightly beaten**
- ☐ **1^1/4 cups/315 mL/10 fl oz buttermilk or milk**

1 Cook bacon in a nonstick frying pan over a medium heat for 3-4 minutes or until crisp. Remove bacon from pan and drain on absorbent kitchen paper.

2 Place corn meal (polenta), flour, baking powder, sugar, salt, Parmesan cheese and butter in a food processor and process until mixture resembles fine bread crumbs.

3 Combine eggs and milk and, with machine running, pour into corn meal mixture and process until just combined and batter is smooth. Take care not to overmix. Stir in bacon.

4 Spoon batter into three medium terracotta flowerpots lined with well-greased aluminium foil. Place on a baking tray and bake for 25-30 minutes or until golden.

Cook's tip: The size of the flowerpots you use will affect the number of loaves you produce.

PIZZA BREAD

Serves 4
Oven temperature 190°C, 375°F, Gas 5

- ☐ **1^1/2 cups/185 g/6 oz flour**
- ☐ **^{1}/2 cup/60 g/2 oz rye or wholemeal flour**
- ☐ **1 teaspoon baking powder**
- ☐ **1 teaspoon bicarbonate of soda**
- ☐ **90 g/3 oz butter, melted**
- ☐ **^{3}/4-1 cup/185-250 mL/6-8 fl oz buttermilk**
- ☐ **^{1}/4 cup/60 mL/2 fl oz tomato paste (purée)**
- ☐ **2 tablespoons chopped fresh oregano or 2 teaspoons dried oregano**
- ☐ **freshly ground black pepper**
- ☐ **100 g/3^1/2 oz thinly sliced salami**
- ☐ **1 onion, thinly sliced**
- ☐ **1 tomato, thinly sliced**
- ☐ **4 tablespoons grated fresh Parmesan cheese**
- ☐ **3 tablespoons pine nuts**
- ☐ **200 g/6^1/2 oz mozzarella cheese, grated**

1 Sift together flour and rye flour, baking powder and bicarbonate of soda into a mixing bowl. Add butter and buttermilk and mix to form a soft dough.

2 Turn onto a floured surface and knead lightly until smooth. Press into a greased 22 x 30 cm/8^3/4 x 12 in Swiss roll tin.

3 Spread dough with tomato paste, sprinkle with oregano and black pepper, then top with salami, onion, tomato, Parmesan cheese, pine nuts and mozzarella cheese. Bake for 15-20 minutes or until topping is golden and base is cooked through.

CHEESE STRAWS

Makes 40
Oven temperature 200°C, 400°F, Gas 6

- ☐ **375 g/12 oz prepared or ready-rolled puff pastry**
- ☐ **60 g/2 oz grated tasty cheese (mature Cheddar)**
- ☐ **60 g/2 oz grated fresh Parmesan cheese**
- ☐ **1 teaspoon paprika**

1 Roll out pastry to 3 mm/^{1}/8 in thick. Combine cheeses with paprika and sprinkle over half the pastry. Fold uncovered pastry half over cheese mixture, then roll together firmly, using a rolling pin.

2 Cut into strips 1 cm/^{1}/2 in wide and twist. Place on wet baking trays and bake for 10 minutes or until puffed and golden.

PANCAKE STACKS

Stacked with your favourite savoury or sweet filling, pancakes are a fun treat for breakfast, lunch or supper.

Serves 4

- ☐ **1 cup/125 g/4 oz self-raising flour**
- ☐ **1¹/₂ tablespoons caster sugar**
- ☐ **¹/₂ teaspoon salt**
- ☐ **1 egg, lightly beaten**
- ☐ **³/₄ cup/185 mL/6 fl oz milk**
- ☐ **60 g/2 oz butter, melted**

1   Place flour, sugar and salt in a food processor or blender. Combine egg, milk and butter and, with machine running, pour into flour mixture and process until smooth.

2   Cook spoonfuls of mixture in a greased frying pan, over a medium-high heat, until bubbles form on the surface. Turn and cook until golden brown. Serve warm and stacked with filling of your choice.

Asparagus and Chicken Pancakes: This is a delectable savoury filling for pancakes. Melt 15 g/¹/₂ oz butter in a small saucepan, stir in 4 teaspoons flour and cook over a medium heat for 1 minute. Remove pan from heat and gradually blend in ¹/₂ cup/125 mL/4 fl oz milk and ¹/₂ cup/125 mL/4 fl oz chicken stock. Return pan to heat and cook, stirring constantly, until sauce boils and mixture thickens. Stir in 250 g/8 oz chopped cooked chicken, 125 g/4 oz chopped and blanched asparagus spears, ¹/₂ teaspoon paprika and freshly ground black pepper to taste. Top pancakes with chicken mixture.

Sweet serving suggestions: Pancakes are delicious topped with any of the following: sugar and freshly squeezed lemon juice; honey and butter; vanilla ice cream, chocolate fudge sauce and toasted hazelnuts.

Pancake Stacks, Pizza Bread

Puff pastry always gives a spectacular result and no more so than in these mini croissants. The secret with these savoury delights is in the shape. Follow the step-by-step instructions to make the quickest and tastiest treats ever.

MINI ASPARAGUS AND CHEESE CROISSANTS

Makes 12
Oven temperature 220°C, 425°F, Gas 7

- ☐ **250 g/8 oz prepared or ready-rolled puff pastry sheets**
- ☐ **1 egg, lightly beaten with 1 tablespoon water**

ASPARAGUS AND CHEESE FILLING
- ☐ **4 stalks fresh asparagus, blanched and finely chopped**
- ☐ **60 g/2 oz Gruyère cheese, grated**
- ☐ **¹/₄ teaspoon paprika**
- ☐ **freshly ground black pepper**

1   To make filling, place asparagus, cheese, paprika and black pepper to taste in a bowl and mix to combine.
2   Roll out pastry to 3 mm/¹/₈ in thick and cut into 10 cm/4 in strips. Cut each strip into triangles with 10 cm/4 in bases.
3   Place a little filling across the base of each triangle, roll up from the base and mould into a croissant shape. Brush with egg mixture.
4   Place croissants on greased baking trays and bake for 12-15 minutes or until puffed and golden. Serve hot or cold.

Ham and Cheese Croissants: Melt 15 g/¹/₂ oz butter in a frying pan and cook 100 g/3¹/₂ oz finely chopped ham and 2 finely chopped spring onions over a medium heat for 3-4 minutes or until onions are soft. Remove from heat, stir in 2 teaspoons finely chopped parsley and season to taste with black pepper. Set filling aside to cool, then assemble, sprinkling filling with 45 g/1¹/₂ oz tasty cheese (mature Cheddar), and cook as for Mini Asparagus and Cheese Croissants.

Chocolate Croissants: As a filling for these delicious morsels use 45 g/1¹/₂ oz grated milk or dark chocolate. Place a little chocolate across the base of each triangle, roll up from the base and mould into a croissant shape. Brush with egg mixture and cook as for Mini Asparagus and Cheese Croissants.

Roll out pastry to 3 mm/¹/₈ in thick and cut into 10 cm/4 in strips. Cut each strip into triangles with 10 cm/4 in bases.

Place a little filling across the base of each triangle and roll up from the base.

Mould each roll into a croissant shape and place on greased baking trays.

CHILLI SOUP BISCUITS

Makes 16 biscuits
Oven temperature 220°C, 425°F, Gas 7

- [ ] **2 rashers bacon, finely chopped**
- [ ] **2 cups/250 g/8 oz flour**
- [ ] **3 teaspoons baking powder**
- [ ] **¹/₂ teaspoon salt**
- [ ] **90 g/3 oz butter**
- [ ] **90 g/3 oz grated tasty cheese (mature Cheddar)**
- [ ] **2 small red chillies, seeded and finely chopped**
- [ ] **²/₃ cup/170 mL/5¹/₂ fl oz milk**
- [ ] **30 g/1 oz butter, melted**

1 Cook bacon in a nonstick frying pan over a medium high heat for 3-4 minutes or until crisp. Remove from pan and drain on absorbent kitchen paper.
2 Sift together flour, baking powder and salt into a mixing bowl. Rub in butter with fingertips until mixture resembles coarse bread crumbs.
3 Stir bacon, cheese and chillies into flour mixture. Add milk and mix to form a soft dough. Turn onto a floured surface and knead lightly with fingertips until smooth.
4 Using heel of hand, gently press dough out to 1 cm/¹/₂ in thick. Cut out rounds using a 5 cm/2 in pastry cutter. Place on a greased baking tray and brush with melted butter. Bake for 12-15 minutes or until golden brown. Remove from tray and cool on a wire rack or serve warm spread with butter.

HERB ROLLS

Spring onions and herbs have been added to this soda bread recipe. The dough is then formed into rolls to make the quickest herb-flavoured rolls ever.

Makes 12 rolls
Oven temperature 180°C, 350°F, Gas 4

- [ ] **90 g/3 oz butter**
- [ ] **8 spring onions, finely chopped**
- [ ] **2¹/₂ cups/315 g/10 oz flour**
- [ ] **1 cup/125 g/4 oz self-raising flour**
- [ ] **3 teaspoons baking powder**
- [ ] **¹/₂ teaspoon bicarbonate of soda**
- [ ] **4 teaspoons sugar**
- [ ] **1 tablespoon finely chopped fresh parsley**
- [ ] **1 tablespoon finely chopped fresh basil**
- [ ] **¹/₂ cup/125 mL/4 fl oz buttermilk or milk**
- [ ] **3 eggs, lightly beaten**
- [ ] **1 egg, beaten with 1¹/₂ teaspoons olive oil**

1 Melt butter in a frying pan and cook spring onions over a medium heat for 2-3 minutes or until onions are soft. Remove from heat and set aside.
2 Sift together flour and self-raising flour, baking powder and bicarbonate of soda into a large mixing bowl. Stir in sugar, parsley and basil. Combine milk, eggs and onion mixture and mix into flour mixture to form a firm dough.
3 Turn onto a floured surface and knead lightly until smooth. Divide dough into twelve portions and roll each into a ball then place on greased and floured baking trays. Brush each roll with egg and oil mixture and bake for 30-35 minutes or until cooked through.

SODA BREAD

A loaf for when you need bread unexpectedly. Soda bread is made with bicarbonate of soda rather than yeast so requires no rising. It is best eaten slightly warm.

Serves 8
Oven temperature 200°C, 400°F, Gas 6

- [ ] **4 cups/500 g/1 lb flour**
- [ ] **1 teaspoon bicarbonate of soda**
- [ ] **1 teaspoon salt**
- [ ] **45 g/1¹/₂ oz butter**
- [ ] **2 cups/500 mL/16 fl oz buttermilk or milk**

1 Sift together flour, bicarbonate of soda and salt into a mixing bowl. Rub in butter using fingertips until mixture resembles coarse bread crumbs. Make a well in the centre of the flour mixture and pour in milk. Using a round-ended knife, mix to form a soft dough.
2 Turn dough onto a floured surface and knead lightly until smooth. Shape into an 18 cm/7 in round and place on a greased and floured baking tray. Score dough into eighths using a sharp knife. Dust lightly with flour and bake for 35-40 minutes or until loaf sounds hollow when tapped on the base.
Serving suggestion: Wonderful spread with lashings of treacle or golden syrup.

Chilli Soup Biscuits, Herb Rolls, Soda Bread

herb HINTS

Herbs have been used for centuries to flavour breads and spreads. Popular fresh herbs for flavouring baked goods are parsley, chives and basil. Dried herbs include rosemary, oregano and marjoram.

Basil: Originating from India, this annual with peppery, clove-scented leaves grows well in a sunny place. Use on pizzas, or mix with butter to make a delicious spread for a tomato sandwich.

Chives: A member of the onion family, chives have hollow onion-flavoured leaves and attractive edible mauve flowers. Their flavour makes them ideal for combining with other herbs and they are a tasty addition to savoury breads and scones.

Marjoram: This herb with its fresh fragrant aroma teams well with tomatoes and is delicious as a pizza flavouring.

Oregano: A form of wild marjoram, oregano is used fresh or dried and is characteristic of Mediterranean cooking. Sprinkle over pizza before cooking or even add it to the dough.

Parsley: A native to the Mediterranean region this would have to be the most popular of all herbs. Add to savoury and herb breads, rolls and scones and use parsley butter as an alternative to garlic butter.

Rosemary: Used either fresh or dried, rosemary has a distinctive flavour that is a pleasant addition to savoury baked goods. You will find that a little goes a long way, so use with caution and chop finely before using in breads, scones or as a flavouring for butter.

COFFEE

Coffee is one of the most popular beverages, and also plays an important role as a flavouring for cakes, biscuits, slices and sweets. If you are using instant coffee powder, dissolve it first in hot water before adding to any mixture. This will ensure you don't end up with specks of undissolved coffee in the finished product.

Left: Little Coffee Cakes, Coffee Oat and Date Cake, Mocha Fudge (all recipes page 40)

nutty KNOWLEDGE

Whether used whole, chopped, slivered or ground, nuts are an important and interesting addition to baked goods. Toasting, grinding and chopping are the most important techniques to correctly master.

Toasting nuts: This increases the flavour of the nuts. Place on a baking tray and heat at 180°C/ 350°F/Gas 4 for 5 minutes, shaking the tray once or twice. Take care not to burn. Remove when nuts are just golden.

To toast nuts in the microwave oven: Place 250 g/ 8 oz nuts in a microwave-safe glass or ceramic dish and cook on HIGH (100%) for 2-3 minutes. Do not add any oil or fat and watch the nuts carefully as the centre toasts before the outsides become brown.

Grinding and chopping: The consistency of chopped or ground nuts is important to the success of a recipe. Ground nuts should be a powder not a paste. Particular care should be taken when using a food processor or grinder as they chop nuts very quickly. When chopping nuts in a food processor use the pulse button and only chop about 60 g/2 oz nuts at a time. When grinding nuts use a special nut mill, coffee grinder or food processor. Only grind a few nuts at a time so that as little oil as possible is released and you do not overwork the nuts and make a paste. When a recipe uses flour or sugar, a little added to the nuts during processing will help to avoid overworking.

LITTLE COFFEE CAKES

Makes 24
Oven temperature 200°C, 400°F, Gas 6

- ☐ 1^1/$_2$ cups/185 g/6 oz self-raising flour, sifted
- ☐ ^{1}/$_2$ cup/100 g/3^1/$_2$ oz caster sugar
- ☐ 2 eggs, lightly beaten
- ☐ 2 teaspoons instant coffee powder dissolved in 2 teaspoons hot water, cooled
- ☐ 60 g/2 oz butter, melted
- ☐ ^{1}/$_2$ cup/125 mL/4 fl oz milk

COFFEE ICING
- ☐ 1^1/$_2$ cups/220 g/7 oz icing sugar, sifted
- ☐ 2 teaspoons butter, softened
- ☐ 1 teaspoon instant coffee powder dissolved in 1^1/$_2$ teaspoons hot water, cooled
- ☐ chocolate sprinkles or coffee beans

1 Place flour, sugar, eggs, coffee mixture, butter and milk in a large mixing bowl and beat until ingredients are well combined and mixture is smooth.
2 Spoon batter into greased patty pans (tartlet tins) and bake for 10-12 minutes or until cakes are well risen and cooked when tested with a skewer. Remove cakes from pans (tins) and cool on a wire rack.
3 To make icing, place icing sugar, butter and coffee mixture in a bowl and beat to make an icing of a spreadable consistency. Spread icing over cold cakes and top with chocolate sprinkles or coffee beans.

MOCHA FUDGE

This coffee-flavoured chocolate fudge is sure to become a family favourite.

Makes 30 squares

- ☐ 500 g/1 lb dark chocolate
- ☐ 1 cup/250 mL/8 fl oz sweetened condensed milk
- ☐ 30 g/1 oz butter
- ☐ 3 teaspoons instant coffee

Place chocolate, condensed milk, butter and coffee in a small saucepan and cook, stirring, over a low heat until mixture is smooth. Pour fudge into an aluminium foil-lined 20 cm/8 in square cake tin and refrigerate for 2 hours or until set. Cut into squares.

COFFEE OAT AND DATE CAKE

Sprinkled with a crunchy topping before baking this cake requires no icing.

Makes a 23 cm/9 in square cake
Oven temperature 180°C, 350°F, Gas 4

- ☐ 125 g/4 oz butter, softened
- ☐ 4 teaspoons instant coffee powder dissolved in 4 teaspoons hot water, cooled
- ☐ ^{3}/$_4$ cup/170 g/5^1/$_2$ oz caster sugar
- ☐ 2 eggs, lightly beaten
- ☐ 1^1/$_2$ cups/185 g/6 oz self-raising flour, sifted
- ☐ ^{1}/$_2$ cup/125 mL/4 fl oz buttermilk or milk

DATE AND OAT TOPPING
- ☐ 200 g/6^1/$_2$ oz pitted dates, chopped
- ☐ ^{2}/$_3$ cup/170 mL/5^1/$_2$ fl oz water
- ☐ 1^1/$_2$ tablespoons caster sugar
- ☐ 3 tablespoons rolled oats
- ☐ 1 tablespoon soft brown sugar
- ☐ 2 tablespoons self-raising flour
- ☐ 30 g/1 oz butter, melted
- ☐ 1 tablespoon chopped walnuts

1 To make topping, place dates, water and caster sugar in a saucepan and cook over a medium heat for 3-4 minutes or until dates are soft and mixture thickens slightly. Remove from heat and set aside to cool. Place oats, sugar and flour in a bowl and stir in butter and walnuts. Set aside.
2 Place butter, coffee mixture, sugar, eggs, flour and milk in a large mixing bowl and beat until all ingredients are combined and mixture is smooth. Spoon batter into a greased and lined 23 cm/9 in square cake tin and top with date mixture, then sprinkle over oat mixture. Bake for 40-45 minutes or until cake is cooked when tested with a skewer. Stand cake in tin for 10 minutes before turning onto a wire rack to cool.

COFFEE SANDWICH CAKE

Layers of light sponge sandwiched together with a liqueur cream and topped with a coffee icing. All this cake needs is a wonderful cup of coffee to accompany it.

Makes an 18 cm/7 in sandwich cake
Oven temperature 160°C, 325°F, Gas 3

- ☐ **250 g/8 oz butter, softened**
- ☐ **1 cup/220 g/7 oz caster sugar**
- ☐ **6 eggs, lightly beaten**
- ☐ **2 cups/250 g/8 oz self-raising flour, sifted**
- ☐ **4 teaspoons baking powder**

COFFEE ICING
- ☐ **60 g/2 oz butter, softened**
- ☐ **³/₄ cup/125 g/4 oz icing sugar, sifted**
- ☐ **¹/₂ teaspoon ground cinnamon**
- ☐ **2 teaspoons instant coffee powder dissolved in 2 teaspoons hot water, cooled**

LIQUEUR CREAM
- ☐ **1 tablespoon Tia Maria**
- ☐ **¹/₂ cup/125 mL/4 fl oz cream (double), whipped**

1 Place butter and sugar in a food processor and process until creamy. Add eggs, flour and baking powder and process until all ingredients are combined. Spoon batter into two greased and lined 18 cm/7 in sandwich tins and bake for 30-35 minutes or until golden. Turn onto a wire rack to cool.

2 To make icing, place butter, icing sugar, cinnamon and coffee mixture in a food processor and process until fluffy.

3 To make filling, fold Tia Maria into whipped cream. Spread filling over one cake and top with remaining cake. Spread icing over top of cake.

Cook's tip: You can use any coffee-flavoured liqueur in place of Tia Maria, or for a nonalcoholic version dissolve 1 teaspoon instant coffee powder in 1 teaspoon hot water, cool, then fold into cream.

Coffee Sandwich Cake

The dough for these coffee-flavoured biscuits is similar to a shortbread – making it perfect for piping. Follow the step-by-step instructions and see just how easy they are to make.

COFFEE KISSES

Makes 25
Oven temperature 180°C, 350°F, Gas 4

- ☐ **250 g/8 oz butter, softened**
- ☐ **²/₃ cup/100 g/3¹/₂ oz icing sugar, sifted**
- ☐ **2 teaspoons instant coffee powder dissolved in 1 tablespoon hot water, cooled**
- ☐ **2 cups/250 g/8 oz flour, sifted**
- ☐ **45 g/1¹/₂ oz dark chocolate, melted**
- ☐ **icing sugar**

1 Place butter and icing sugar in a large mixing bowl and beat until light and fluffy. Stir in coffee mixture and flour.
2 Spoon mixture into a piping bag fitted with a medium star nozzle and pipe 2 cm/³/₄ in rounds of mixture 2 cm/³/₄ in apart on greased baking trays. Bake for 10-12 minutes or until lightly browned. Stand on trays for 5 minutes before removing to wire racks to cool completely.
3 Join biscuits with a little melted chocolate, then dust with icing sugar.

Spoon mixture into a piping bag fitted with a medium star nozzle.

Pipe 2 cm/³/₄ in rounds of mixture 2 cm/³/₄ in apart on greased baking trays.

Join biscuits with a little melted chocolate, then dust with icing sugar.

BAKING SECRETS

What happens when you make a cake?
One of the secrets to producing wonderful cakes
and biscuits is to understand why certain
techniques are used.

MAKING THE CAKE

🍂 Many recipes begin by creaming the butter and sugar. This is an important process as little bubbles of air are trapped in the mixture and it is this air which helps to produce a light-textured cake.

🍂 The butter should be softened for the creaming process and the mixture beaten until it is creamy and fluffy and almost doubled in volume.

🍂 Creaming can be done with a balloon whisk, wooden spoon, electric mixer or food processor.

🍂 After the creaming process an egg or eggs are often added to the mixture. The egg white forms a layer around each bubble of air and as the cake cooks the egg white coagulates and forms a wall around each bubble, preventing the bubbles from bursting and so ruining the cake.

🍂 As the cake cooks, the air bubbles expand and the cake rises.

🍂 As the air bubbles are expanding, the gluten in the flour is also stretching. This will continue until the gluten loses its elasticity.

🍂 Do not open the oven door until at least halfway through the recommended cooking time or the rising process is interrupted. With the sudden drop in temperature the cake stops expanding and it sinks because there is no structure to support it.

🍂 The oven should be preheated to the correct temperature before placing the cake in to cook.

🍂 If baking more than one cake, arrange the tins so that they do not touch each other or the sides of the oven.

🍂 Filling the cake tin is an important step towards a successful result. If your batter is soft it can be poured into the cake tin, however a firm batter should be spooned into the tin and spread out evenly using a spatula. For light batters, only half to two-thirds fill the tin; heavy batters can fill as much as three-quarters of the tin.

IS THE CAKE COOKED?

🍂 Test your cake just before the end of the cooking time. To test the cake, insert a skewer into the thickest part of the cake. If it comes away clean, your cake is cooked. If there is still cake mixture on the skewer, cook for 5 minutes longer then test again.

🍂 Alternately, you can gently press the top of the cake with your fingertips. When cooked, the depression will spring back quickly.

When the cake starts to leave the side of the tin this is another indication that the cake is cooked.

COOLING THE CAKE

You will find that a freshly baked cake is very fragile. Allow a cake to cool for a short time in the tin before turning onto a wire rack to cool completely.

Before turning out a cake, loosen the sides with a spatula or palette knife. Then turn the cake onto a wire rack to cool and immediately invert on to a second wire rack so that the top of the cake is not marked with indentations from the rack. If you do not have a second wire rack, invert the cake onto a clean cloth on your hand then turn it back onto the wire rack.

STORING BAKED PRODUCTS

Allow cakes to cool completely before placing in an airtight container, or condensation will accumulate in the container and cause the cake to go mouldy.

Keeping times for cakes vary depending on the ingredients used. A fatless sponge will only stay fresh for 1-2 days while one made with fat will keep fresh for 3 days. Cakes made using the creaming method usually keep fresh for up to a week. Light fruit cakes keep for 2-3 weeks and heavy rich fruit cakes will store for a month or more.

Most undecorated cakes can be frozen successfully. Wrap the cake in freezer wrap or place in a freezer bag and seal. If freezing several cakes, wrap each separately or place freezer wrap or waxed paper between cakes so that they are easy to remove.

To thaw a frozen cake, leave in package and thaw at room temperature. Large cakes will take 3-4 hours to thaw, layer cakes 1-2 hours and small cakes about 30 minutes.

PREPARING THE CAKE TINS

To grease and flour a cake tin: Using a pastry brush lightly brush cake tin with melted butter or margarine, then sprinkle with flour and shake to coat evenly. Invert tin on work surface and tap gently to remove excess flour.

To grease and line a round cake tin: Place cake tin on a large piece of baking paper and using a pencil trace around the base, then cut out shape. Grease tin and line with paper.

To line a deep cake tin: A deep cake tin should be lined on the bottom and sides. Use a double-thickness folded strip of baking paper 5 cm/2 in higher than the cake tin and long enough to fit around the tin and to overlap by about 2.5 cm/1 in. On the folded edge turn up about 2.5 cm/1 in and crease, then using scissors snip at regular intervals across the margin as far as the fold. Cut out a piece of baking paper to line the base of the tin as described above. Grease the tin and place the strip inside the tin with the snipped margin lying flat on the base of the tin. Ensure that the ends overlap so that the sides are completely covered by the paper. Place the base piece of baking paper in the tin to cover the snipped margin.

To line a loaf tin: Cut a strip of baking paper the width of the base of the tin and long enough to come up the shorter sides of the tin and overlap by 2.5 cm/1 in. Grease the tin and line with the paper. When the cake is cooked the unlined sides can be loosened with a knife and the paper ends are used to lift out the cake.

SUGAR AND SPICE

Sugar and spice and all things nice. Sugar is one of the most important ingredients used in baked products, but it is a relatively recent addition to the pantry shelf. Not until the seventeenth century was sugar plentiful. Before this time honey, sweet fruits and fruit syrups were the main sweeteners used.

Right: Eggless Gingerbread Cake, Ginger Crunch, Shortbread Swirls (all recipes on page 48)

special SPICES

Spices are the baker's best friend. A teaspoon here and a pinch there can add that something extra to any cake, biscuit or slice. Popular spices used in baking are allspice, cardamom, cinnamon, cloves, ginger and vanilla.

Allspice: Tasting of a mixture of cloves, cinnamon and nutmeg, this spice when ground is a popular ingredient in any recipe with apples.

Cardamom: Belonging to the ginger family, cardamom will only grow in hot climates. This spice with a sweet camphor-like flavour goes well with fruit and is popular as an ingredient in bread and yeast cakes.

Cinnamon: Cinnamon is the bark of a tree belonging to the laurel family. The bark is sold in small quills (cinnamon sticks) or as a powder. Used in many baked products it is a standard spice for any pantry.

Cloves: Dark, pungent and exotic, cloves are the flower buds of the clove tree. Native to the Spice Islands, cloves are available whole or ground. Use ground cloves cautiously as they tend to taste very strong.

Ginger: With its sweet hot flavour ginger is the perfect spice for baking. Most commonly used as the ground spice, chopped crystallised ginger and ginger in syrup are also tasty additions to cakes and biscuits.

Vanilla: The dark brown pod of vanilla comes from a type of orchid native to South America. Vanilla is an interesting addition to cakes, custards and desserts.

EGGLESS GINGERBREAD CAKE

An eggless cake that is ideal for anyone who cannot eat eggs.

Makes a 20 cm/8 in ring cake
Oven temperature 180°C, 350°F, Gas 4

- ☐ **125 g/4 oz butter, melted**
- ☐ **1/2 cup/125 mL/4 fl oz hot water**
- ☐ **1/2 cup/170 g/5 1/2 oz golden syrup, warmed**
- ☐ **1 cup/125 g/4 oz flour, sifted**
- ☐ **1/2 cup/60 g/2 oz self-raising flour, sifted**
- ☐ **1/2 teaspoon bicarbonate of soda**
- ☐ **4 teaspoons ground ginger**
- ☐ **1/2 teaspoon ground nutmeg**
- ☐ **1/2 cup/90 g/3 oz soft brown sugar**
- ☐ **2 tablespoons desiccated coconut**

LEMON ICING
- ☐ **1 1/2 cups/220 g/7 oz icing sugar, sifted**
- ☐ **15 g/1/2 oz butter, softened**
- ☐ **2 teaspoons lemon juice**
- ☐ **milk**

1   Place butter, water and golden syrup in a large mixing bowl. Stir in flour and self-raising flour, bicarbonate of soda, ginger, nutmeg and sugar and mix to combine all ingredients.
2   Spoon batter into a greased 20 cm/8 in ring cake tin and bake for 35-40 minutes or until cake is cooked when tested with a skewer. Stand cake in tin for 5 minutes before turning onto a wire rack to cool.
3   To make icing, place icing sugar in a mixing bowl, mix in butter, lemon juice and enough milk to make an icing of a spreadable consistency. Spread icing over cold cake and sprinkle with coconut.

STORING SPICES

Spices should be stored in sealed containers at room temperature in a cool dark place. Whole spices will keep about a year and ground spices about six months if stored correctly. It is best to buy small quantities of spice so that they are always fresh. Once their colour and aroma fade they should be discarded. The best indication of quality is the aroma.

GINGER CRUNCH

Makes 30

- ☐ **125 g/4 oz butter**
- ☐ **3/4 cup/185 g/6 oz sugar**
- ☐ **1/2 cup/125 mL/4 fl oz sweetened condensed milk**
- ☐ **4 teaspoons golden syrup**
- ☐ **250 g/8 oz gingernut biscuits, crushed**
- ☐ **60 g/2 oz pecans, finely chopped**
- ☐ **2 tablespoons finely chopped glacé ginger or stem ginger in syrup**

1   Place butter, sugar, condensed milk and golden syrup in a small saucepan and cook over a medium heat, stirring constantly until mixture is smooth. Bring to the boil, then reduce heat and simmer for 3-4 minutes or until mixture thickens slightly.
2   Place biscuits, pecans and glacé ginger in a bowl, pour in condensed milk mixture and mix until well combined. Press mixture into a lined, shallow 23 cm/9 in square cake tin and refrigerate until set. Cut into bars.

SHORTBREAD SWIRLS

Melt-in-the-mouth bite-sized shortbread biscuits.

Makes 40
Oven temperature 190°C, 375°F, Gas 5

- ☐ **125 g/4 oz butter, chopped**
- ☐ **3/4 cup/125 g/4 oz icing sugar**
- ☐ **1 1/2 cups/185 g/6 oz flour**
- ☐ **1/3 cup/90 g/3 oz sour cream**
- ☐ **4 teaspoons lemon juice**
- ☐ **2 teaspoons finely grated lemon rind**

1   Place butter, icing sugar, flour, sour cream, lemon juice and lemon rind in a food processor and process until smooth.
2   Spoon mixture into a piping bag fitted with a large star nozzle and pipe small swirls of mixture onto greased baking trays. Bake for 10-12 minutes or until lightly golden. Cool biscuits on trays. Dust with icing sugar.

Orange Swirls: Replace lemon juice and rind with orange juice and rind.

China Waterford Wedgwood

GOLDEN WAFFLES

These crisp and golden waffles are a wonderful base for any number of toppings. For something different try one of the variations.

Makes 16 waffles

- ☐ **2 cups/250 g/8 oz flour**
- ☐ **1 cup/125 g/4 oz self-raising flour**
- ☐ **1¹/₂ teaspoons baking powder**
- ☐ **1 teaspoon salt**
- ☐ **¹/₄ cup/60 g/2 oz caster sugar**
- ☐ **2¹/₄ cups/560 mL/18 fl oz milk**
- ☐ **3 eggs, separated**
- ☐ **125 g/4 oz butter, melted**

1 Sift together flour and self-raising flour, baking powder and salt into a mixing bowl. Stir in sugar.
2 Whisk together milk, egg yolks and butter. Make a well in centre of flour mixture and mix in milk mixture until just combined. Beat egg whites until stiff peaks form, then fold into batter.
3 Cook batter in a preheated, greased waffle iron following the manufacturer's instructions. Serve waffles with topping of your choice.

Brown Sugar Waffles: Use soft brown sugar in place of caster sugar.
Citrus Waffles: Mix 1 teaspoon finely grated orange or lemon rind into batter.
Nutty Waffles: Add 90 g/3 oz chopped toasted pecans, walnuts or macadamia nuts to dry ingredients before adding milk mixture. These waffles are great served with caramel sauce.
Banana Waffles: Mix ¹/₂ banana, mashed into batter before folding through egg whites.
Topping suggestions: Serve waffles hot, topped with: butter and golden syrup or honey; berries and cream; ice cream, chocolate or caramel sauce and chopped nuts; jam and cream.

Freeze it: Waffles can be frozen in an airtight freezer bag or container, then reheated in the oven or toaster straight from the freezer.

Golden Waffles

CRUNCHY CARAMEL CAKE

Makes a 23 cm/9 in square cake
Oven temperature 180°C, 350°F, Gas 4

- ☐ **125 g/4 oz butter, softened**
- ☐ **2 tablespoons golden syrup**
- ☐ **$^1/_2$ cup/90 g/3 oz brown sugar**
- ☐ **2 eggs, lightly beaten**
- ☐ **1$^1/_2$ cups/185 g/6 oz self-raising flour, sifted**
- ☐ **$^1/_2$ cup/125 mL/4 fl oz milk**

CRUNCHY TOPPING
- ☐ **$^3/_4$ cup/75 g/2$^1/_2$ oz rolled oats**
- ☐ **$^1/_4$ cup/30 g/1 oz flour**
- ☐ **15 g/$^1/_2$ oz desiccated coconut**
- ☐ **2 tablespoons soft brown sugar**
- ☐ **45 g/1$^1/_2$ oz butter, melted**

CARAMEL FROSTING
- ☐ **60 g/2 oz butter**
- ☐ **1$^1/_2$ cups/220 g/7 oz icing sugar**
- ☐ **1$^1/_2$ tablespoons golden syrup**

1   Place butter, golden syrup, sugar, eggs, flour and milk in a large mixing bowl. Beat well until all ingredients are combined and batter is smooth.

2   Spoon batter into a greased and lined 23 cm/9 in square cake tin and bake for 40-45 minutes or until cake is cooked when tested with a skewer. Stand cake in tin for 10 minutes before turning onto a wire rack to cool completely.

3   To make topping, place rolled oats, flour, coconut and sugar in a bowl and mix to combine. Stir in butter, then spread mixture on a greased baking tray and bake for 10 minutes or until golden and crunchy.

4   To make frosting, place butter in a small mixing bowl and beat until creamy. Add icing sugar and golden syrup and beat until smooth. Spread frosting over cold cake and sprinkle with topping.

SPONGE CAKE

Makes a 20 cm/8 in round sponge
Oven temperature 180°C, 350°F, Gas 4

- ☐ **4 eggs**
- ☐ **1 cup/220 g/7 oz caster sugar**
- ☐ **1$^1/_4$ cups/155 g/5 oz self-raising flour, sifted**
- ☐ **$^1/_2$ cup/125 mL/4 fl oz milk, warm**
- ☐ **15 g/$^1/_2$ oz butter, melted**
- ☐ **3 tablespoons raspberry jam**
- ☐ **$^1/_2$ cup/125 mL/4 fl oz cream (double), whipped**
- ☐ **icing sugar, sifted**
- ☐ **strawberries, to decorate**

1   Place eggs in a large mixing bowl and beat until light and fluffy. Gradually add sugar, beating well after each addition until mixture is thick and creamy.

2   Gently fold flour into egg mixture. Combine milk and butter and fold into egg mixture. Spoon batter into two greased and lined 20 cm/8 in cake tins and bake for 25 minutes or until sponges are golden and spring back when touched with your fingertips. Stand cakes in tins for 5 minutes before turning onto wire racks to cool.

3   Spread one cake with jam and cream, then top with other cake. Sprinkle top of sponge with icing sugar and decorate with strawberries.

Sponge Cake, Crunchy Caramel Cake

SPICED GINGER DROPS

Ginger lovers won't be able to get enough of these spicy cookies.

Makes 30
Oven temperature 180°C, 350°F, Gas 4

- ☐ **1 cup/125 g/4 oz flour, sifted**
- ☐ **¹/₄ teaspoon ground ginger**
- ☐ **¹/₄ teaspoon ground mixed spice**
- ☐ **¹/₄ teaspoon ground cinnamon**
- ☐ **¹/₂ teaspoon bicarbonate of soda**
- ☐ **60 g/2 oz butter, cut into pieces**
- ☐ **¹/₂ cup/90 g/3 oz soft brown sugar**
- ☐ **2¹/₂ tablespoons golden syrup, warmed**
- ☐ **1¹/₂ tablespoons finely chopped glacé ginger or stem ginger in syrup**

1   Place flour, ground ginger, mixed spice, cinnamon and bicarbonate of soda in a large mixing bowl. Rub in butter until mixture resembles fine bread crumbs. Stir in sugar, golden syrup and glacé ginger.
2   Turn dough onto a lightly floured surface and knead to form a soft dough. Roll rounded teaspoons of mixture into balls and place 3 cm/1¹/₄ in apart on greased baking trays. Bake for 10-15 minutes or until golden. Transfer biscuits to wire racks to cool.

Spiced Ginger Drops

The secret to making these heart-shaped pastries is in the way that you fold the pastry. The step-by-step instructions will have you making these delicious morsels in next to no time. Palmiers are a great way to use leftover puff pastry.

PALMIERS

Makes 18
Oven temperature 220°C, 425°F, Gas 7

☐ **170 g/5$^1/_2$ oz prepared or ready-rolled puff pastry sheets**
☐ **15 g/$^1/_2$ oz butter, melted and cooled**
☐ **3 tablespoons demerara sugar**

1 Roll out pastry to a 25 cm/10 in square, 3 mm/$^1/_8$ in thick.
2 Brush with butter and sprinkle with a little sugar. Fold two opposite edges of pastry halfway towards the centre. Sprinkle with a little more sugar and fold, taking edges to the centre. Sprinkle with a little more sugar and fold one half of pastry over the other half. Press lightly to join.
3 Cut pastry length into eighteen slices and place on a greased baking tray. Flatten slightly and bake for 10-15 minutes or until puffed and golden.
Pistachio Palmiers: Combine 15 g/$^1/_2$ oz finely chopped unsalted pistachio nuts and 3 tablespoons soft brown sugar, and sprinkle over pastry in place of demerara sugar.
Almond Palmiers: Combine 3 tablespoons ground almonds, 2 tablespoons caster sugar and 1 teaspoon ground mixed spice and sprinkle over pastry in place of demerara sugar.
Serving suggestion: Try sandwiching the Palmiers together with whipped cream. Delicious!

Brush pastry with butter and sprinkle with sugar, then fold two opposite edges of pastry halfway towards the centre.

Sprinkle with a little more sugar and fold, taking edges to the centre.

Sprinkle with a little more sugar and fold one half of pastry over the other half and press lightly to join. Cut pastry length into 18 slices.

53

THE ICING ON THE CAKE

This selection of easy icings, fillings and toppings will dress up any plain cake to make it into something really special.

CHOCOLATE RIPPLE CREAM

Cream well chilled, with chocolate folded through as soon as it is melted – the secret to this wonderful topping or filling for a chocolate cake or sponge.

Enough to fill and top a 20 cm/8 in cake

- ☐ **100 g/3¹/₂ oz dark chocolate**
- ☐ **1 cup/250 mL/8 fl oz cream (double), well chilled and whipped**

Melt chocolate in a small bowl over a saucepan of simmering water, or melt in the microwave oven on HIGH (100%) for 45 seconds to 1 minute. Fold melted chocolate through chilled cream.

BUTTERSCOTCH FROSTING

Enough to cover a 20 cm/8 in cake

- ☐ **1¹/₂ cups/250 g/8 oz soft brown sugar**
- ☐ **¹/₄ cup/60 mL/2 fl oz milk**
- ☐ **30 g/1 oz butter**
- ☐ **1 cup/155 g/5 oz icing sugar**

Place sugar, milk and butter in a small saucepan and cook, stirring constantly, over a low heat until sugar dissolves. Bring to the boil and boil for 3-4 minutes. Remove from heat and set aside to cool until just warm, then beat in icing sugar until frosting is of a spreadable consistency. Use immediately.

VANILLA BUTTER ICING

Enough to cover a 20 cm/8 in cake or 18 biscuits

- ☐ **1¹/₂ cups/220 g/7 oz icing sugar, sifted**
- ☐ **60 g/2 oz butter**
- ☐ **2 tablespoons boiling water**
- ☐ **¹/₄ teaspoon vanilla essence**
- ☐ **few drops of food colouring (optional)**

Place icing sugar and butter in a bowl and add boiling water. Mix to make a mixture of spreadable consistency, adding a little more water if necessary. Beat in vanilla essence and food colouring if using.
Chocolate Butter Icing: Add ¹/₄ cup/ 30 g/1 oz cocoa powder to icing sugar.
Coffee Butter Icing: Add 1 tablespoon instant coffee powder to boiling water.
Lemon Butter Icing: Omit vanilla essence and add 1-2 teaspoons fresh lemon juice to icing sugar mixture.
Passion Fruit Icing: Replace vanilla essence with 2-3 tablespoons passion fruit pulp. A little more icing sugar may be required to make an icing of spreadable consistency.

MOCK CREAM

Enough to fill a 20 cm/8 in cake

- ☐ **60 g/2 oz butter**
- ☐ **¹/₄ cup/60 g/2 oz caster sugar**
- ☐ **¹/₄ cup/60 mL/2 fl oz boiling water**
- ☐ **¹/₄ teaspoon vanilla essence**

Place butter and sugar in a small bowl and add boiling water. Beat, using an electric mixer, until creamy. Beat in vanilla essence.
Cook's tip: If the mixture curdles, place over a pan of simmering water and continue beating.

CHOCOLATE FUDGE FROSTING

Enough to fill and cover a 20 cm/8 in cake

- ☐ **³/₄ cup/185 g/6 oz caster sugar**
- ☐ **¹/₃ cup/90 mL/3 fl oz evaporated milk**
- ☐ **125 g/4 oz dark chocolate, broken into pieces**
- ☐ **45 g/1¹/₂ oz butter**
- ☐ **¹/₄ teaspoon vanilla essence**

1   Place sugar and evaporated milk in a heavy-based saucepan and cook, stirring, over a low heat until sugar melts. Bring mixture to the boil and simmer stirring constantly for 4 minutes.
2   Remove pan from heat and stir in chocolate. Continue stirring until chocolate melts, then stir in butter and vanilla essence.
3   Transfer frosting to a bowl and set aside to cool. Cover with plastic food wrap and chill until frosting thickens and is of spreadable consistency.

MARSHMALLOW FROSTING

Enough to fill and cover a 20 cm/8 in cake

- ☐ **1 egg white**
- ☐ **2 teaspoons gelatine dissolved in ¹/₂ cup/125 mL/4 fl oz hot water, cooled**
- ☐ **1 cup/155 g/5 oz icing sugar**
- ☐ **flavouring of your choice**
- ☐ **few drops of colouring (optional)**

Beat egg white until stiff peaks form, then continue beating while gradually adding gelatine mixture. Beat in icing sugar and flavouring. Continue beating until frosting is thick.

From left: Butterscotch Frosting, Chocolate Ripple Cream, Vanilla Butter Icing, Mock Cream, Chocolate Fudge Frosting, Marshmallow Frosting

LUNCH BOX TREAT

Give your family a surprise with
these tasty treats. We have chosen
cakes, biscuits and slices that keep well
and stand up to life in a lunch box.
They will also be popular as snacks
after school or after work.

*Left: Lemon and Pistachio Nut Slice,
Iced Nut Squares, Hazelnut Gems
(all recipes page 58)*

HAZELNUT GEMS

These gems are a light meringue made with hazelnuts then sandwiched together with hazelnut spread.

Makes 25
Oven temperature 180°C, 350°F, Gas 4

- ☐ **3 egg whites**
- ☐ **³/₄ cup/170 g/5¹/₂ oz caster sugar**
- ☐ **125 g/4 oz hazelnuts, ground**
- ☐ **¹/₄ cup/30 g/1 oz flour**
- ☐ **125 g/4 oz chocolate hazelnut spread**

1 Place egg whites in a mixing bowl and beat until stiff peaks form. Fold in sugar, hazelnuts and flour.
2 Place teaspoons of mixture 2.5 cm/1 in apart on greased baking trays and bake for 12-15 minutes or until lightly browned. Stand on trays for 5 minutes before transferring to wire racks to cool. Sandwich cold biscuits together with hazelnut spread.

ICED NUT SQUARES

Everyone will be nuts about these no-bake nut squares.

Makes 30 squares

- ☐ **250 g/8 oz plain sweet biscuits, crushed**
- ☐ **¹/₂ cup/90 g/3 oz soft brown sugar**
- ☐ **30 g/1 oz macadamia or brazil nuts, chopped**
- ☐ **2 tablespoons cocoa powder**
- ☐ **1 teaspoon coffee essence**
- ☐ **¹/₄ cup/60 mL/2 fl oz milk**
- ☐ **125 g/4 oz butter, melted**

CHOCOLATE ICING
- ☐ **125 g/4 oz dark chocolate, broken into small pieces**
- ☐ **90 g/3 oz unsalted butter**

1 Place crushed biscuits, sugar, nuts, cocoa powder, coffee essence, milk and butter in a mixing bowl and mix well to combine. Press mixture into a greased and lined shallow 18 x 28 cm/7 x 11 in cake tin and refrigerate until firm.
2 To make icing, place chocolate and butter in a small saucepan and cook over a low heat, stirring constantly, until melted. Spread over mixture in cake tin and refrigerate until icing is set. Cut into squares.

LEMON AND PISTACHIO NUT SLICE

Topped with pistachio nuts and mixed peel this slice tastes as good as it looks.

Makes 30

- ☐ **250 g/8 oz plain sweet biscuits, crushed**
- ☐ **90 g/3 oz pistachio nuts, chopped**
- ☐ **2 teaspoons finely grated lemon rind**
- ☐ **¹/₂ cup/125 mL/4 fl oz sweetened condensed milk**
- ☐ **125 g/4 oz butter, melted**

LEMON PISTACHIO TOPPING
- ☐ **125 g/4 oz cream cheese, softened**
- ☐ **¹/₂ cup/90 g/3 oz icing sugar, sifted**
- ☐ **2 teaspoons lemon juice**
- ☐ **3 tablespoons mixed peel, finely chopped**
- ☐ **1 tablespoon chopped pistachio nuts**

1 Place crushed biscuits, nuts, lemon rind, condensed milk and butter in a mixing bowl and mix to combine. Press mixture into a greased and lined shallow 18 x 28 cm/7 x 11 in cake tin and refrigerate until firm.
2 To make topping, place cream cheese and icing sugar in a mixing bowl and beat until fluffy. Beat in lemon juice and spread over mixture in cake tin. Sprinkle with mixed peel and pistachio nuts. Refrigerate until icing is firm, then cut into bars.

CUTTING CAKE

The best way to cut a delicate cake is to use a long sharp knife. Dip the knife into a jug of hot water, then shake off the water and cut your cake. The blade of the hot knife will melt through the icing and filling and so make a clean cut in the cake that does not tear the delicate structure. Wipe the blade of the knife with a damp cloth before cutting the next slice of cake. Dip the knife in the hot water again as the blade becomes cool.

CHOCOLATE RUM AND RAISIN SLICE

Flavoured with rum essence and topped with a chocolate frosting this slice is made of all the best ingredients.

Makes 25 squares
Oven temperature 180°C, 350°F, Gas 4

- ☐ **1 cup/125 g/4 oz self-raising flour, sifted**
- ☐ **1 tablespoon cocoa powder, sifted**
- ☐ **^{1}/2 cup/100 g/3^1/2 oz caster sugar**
- ☐ **75 g/2^1/2 oz desiccated coconut**
- ☐ **75 g/2^1/2 oz raisins, chopped**
- ☐ **125 g/4 oz butter, melted**
- ☐ **1 teaspoon rum essence**
- ☐ **2 tablespoons grated dark chocolate**

CHOCOLATE FROSTING
- ☐ **1 cup/155 g/5 oz icing sugar**
- ☐ **4 teaspoons cocoa powder**
- ☐ **15 g/^{1}/2 oz butter, softened**
- ☐ **4 teaspoons of water**

1   Place flour, cocoa powder, sugar, coconut and raisins in a large mixing bowl. Combine butter and rum essence, pour into dry ingredients and mix well to combine.

2   Press mixture into a greased and lined 23 cm/9 in square cake tin and bake for 20-25 minutes or until firm. Remove from oven and allow to cool in tin.

3   To make frosting, place icing sugar and cocoa powder into a mixing bowl. Add butter and water and beat until a spreadable consistency.

4   Remove slice from tin and spread with frosting. Sprinkle with grated chocolate. Cover and refrigerate until frosting is firm. Cut into squares.

Chocolate Rum and Raisin Slice

Tiles Country Floors *Plate, cup and saucer* Villeroy & Boch *Coffee grinder* Butler & Co

FRUITY CEREAL SLICE

Dried fruit, rice bubbles, coconut, nuts and honey – just reading the ingredients you know that this slice is going to be delicious.

Makes 30

- ☐ 3 cups/90 g/3 oz unsweetened puffed rice cereal
- ☐ 1 cup/45 g/1^1/$_2$ oz bran flakes, crumbled
- ☐ 125 g/4 oz slivered almonds, toasted
- ☐ 125 g/4 oz dried apricots, chopped
- ☐ 100 g/3^1/$_2$ oz glacé pineapple, chopped
- ☐ 100 g/3^1/$_2$ oz glacé ginger or stem ginger in syrup, chopped
- ☐ 90 g/3 oz raisins, chopped
- ☐ 170 g/5^1/$_2$ oz sultanas
- ☐ 125 g/4 oz butter
- ☐ ^{1}/$_2$ cup/125 mL/4 fl oz cream (double)
- ☐ ^{1}/$_2$ cup/170 g/5^1/$_2$ oz honey
- ☐ ^{1}/$_3$ cup/90 g/3 oz demerara sugar

1   Place rice cereal, bran flakes, almonds, apricots, pineapple, ginger, raisins and sultanas in a large mixing bowl and set aside.

2   Combine butter, cream, honey and sugar in a saucepan and cook over a low heat, stirring constantly, until sugar dissolves and butter melts. Bring to the boil, then reduce heat and simmer for 5 minutes or until mixture thickens slightly.

3   Pour honey mixture into dry ingredients and mix well to combine. Press mixture into a greased and lined shallow 18 x 28 cm/7 x 11 in cake tin. Refrigerate until firm, then cut into squares.

DATE BARS

Studded with dates and pecans, this slice is a great lunch box filler.

Makes 30
Oven temperature 180°C, 350°F, Gas 4

- ☐ ^{3}/$_4$ cup/185 mL/6 fl oz evaporated milk
- ☐ 125 g/4 oz pitted dates, chopped
- ☐ 125 g/4 oz butter, softened
- ☐ ^{1}/$_2$ cup/100 g/3^1/$_2$ oz caster sugar
- ☐ 1 teaspoon vanilla essence
- ☐ 1 cup/125 g/4 oz self-raising flour, sifted
- ☐ 60 g/2 oz pecans, chopped

1   Place evaporated milk in a saucepan and cook over a low heat until just boiling, then remove pan from heat. Place dates in a bowl, pour hot milk over and set aside to cool.

2   Combine butter, sugar and vanilla essence in a large mixing bowl and beat until light and fluffy. Mix flour and date mixture, alternately, into butter mixture, then fold in pecans. Spoon mixture into a greased and lined 23 cm/9 in square cake tin and bake for 25-30 minutes or until firm. Stand in tin 5 minutes before turning onto a wire rack to cool. Cut into bars.

FLOUR SUBSTITUTES

If the recipe calls for:	You can use:
All-purpose flour	White flour
Cake flour	Flour or a mixture of flour and cornflour. For 1 cup/125 g/4 oz flour, replace 2 tablespoons with cornflour, sift the flours together to ensure that they are well mixed
Wholewheat flour	Wholemeal flour

Date Bars, Fruity Cereal Slice

flour POWER

Flour provides the structure that holds the cake together. The most common flour is that milled from wheat, but there are also other flours that can be used in baking to give interesting and varying results.

Flour: This flour is a blend of hard and soft wheat flours. The proportions tend to vary a little from country to country. For example in America, where flour is known as all-purpose flour, the proportion of hard wheat flour is usually greater than in flours produced in Europe. The American cake and pastry flours are soft wheat flours.

Self-raising flour: This is flour with baking powder and salt added. You can make your own self-raising flour if you wish by sifting flour with baking powder – for 1 cup/125 g/4 oz flour allow 1 teaspoon baking powder.

Wholemeal flour: This flour uses the whole grain so retains all the flavour and nutrients of the grain. Wholemeal flour has a higher bran content than flour which reduces the effectiveness of the gluten. Therefore baked goods made with wholemeal flour tend to have a heavier, more dense texture.

❧ Sifting flour is important as it adds air to the mixture, giving lightness to your cake. To sift flour, hold sieve well above the bowl so the flour gets a good airing as it falls into the bowl.

❧ Flour should be stored in an airtight container in a cool, dark place. Due to its moisture and fat content flour will eventually go rancid.

DANISH PASTRIES

Serve these easy Danish Pastries for breakfast or brunch, with morning coffee or afternoon tea. No matter what the occasion, they are sure to impress.

APRICOT DANISH PASTRIES

Makes 8
Oven temperature 220°C, 425°F, Gas 7

☐ **300 g/9^1/$_2$ oz prepared or ready-rolled puff pastry sheets**
☐ **8 canned apricot halves, drained**
☐ **1 quantity Apricot Glaze (below)**

1   Roll out pastry to 3 mm/^{1}/$_8$ in thick. Cut into eight 10 cm/4 in squares. Make four 5 cm/2 in cuts, starting from each corner and cutting towards the centre of each pastry square.
2   Fold one half of each corner to centre and place an apricot over the top. Repeat with remaining pastry squares and apricots.
3   Place pastries on greased baking trays and bake for 15-20 minutes or until puffed and golden. Brush hot pastries with glaze. Cool pastries on a wire rack.

SWEET CHEESE PASTRIES

Makes 8
Oven temperature 220°C, 425°F, Gas 7

☐ **300 g/9^1/$_2$ oz prepared or ready-rolled puff pastry sheets**
☐ **1 tablespoon water**
☐ **1 quantity Apricot Glaze (below)**

CREAM CHEESE FILLING
☐ **200 g/6^1/$_2$ oz cream cheese**
☐ **1 egg yolk**
☐ **2 tablespoons caster sugar**

1   To make filling, place cream cheese, egg yolk and sugar in a food processor or blender and process until smooth.
2   Roll out pastry to 3 mm/^{1}/$_8$ in thick and cut into eight 12 cm/4^3/$_4$ in squares. Spread filling over half the pastry rectangle leaving a 1 cm/^{1}/$_2$ in border. Brush edge with a little water and fold pastry over to enclose filling. Press edges firmly together to seal. Cut six slits 3 cm/1^1/$_4$ in in length along joined edges of pastry. Repeat with remaining pastry rectangles and filling.
3   Place pastries on greased baking trays and bake for 15-20 minutes or until puffed and golden. Brush hot pastries with glaze. Cool pastries on a wire rack.

CHERRY SQUARES

Makes 8
Oven temperature 220°C, 425°F, Gas 7

☐ **300 g/9^1/$_2$ oz prepared or ready-rolled puff pastry sheets**
☐ **1 quantity Apricot Glaze (below)**

CHERRY FILLING
☐ **750 g/1^1/$_2$ lb bottled, pitted morello cherries, drained**
☐ **^{1}/$_4$ cup/60 g/2 oz caster sugar**
☐ **1 teaspoon ground cinnamon**

1   To make filling, combine cherries, sugar and cinnamon in a bowl. Set aside.
2   Roll out pastry to 3 mm/^{1}/$_8$ in thick and cut into eight 12 cm/4^3/$_4$ in squares. Roll in edges to form a narrow rim, then place a spoonful of filling in centre of each pastry square.
3   Place pastries on greased baking trays and bake for 15-20 minutes or until puffed and golden. Brush hot pastries with glaze. Cool pastries on a wire rack.

APRICOT GLAZE

☐ **^{1}/$_2$ cup/155 g/5 oz apricot jam**
☐ **4 teaspoons water**

Place jam and water in a small saucepan and cook over a high heat until mixture boils. Remove from heat and use as required.

From top: Sweet Cheese Pastries, Apricot Danish Pastries, Cherry Squares

HEALTHY IDEAS

Good tastes that are full of goodness!
Enjoy these cakes, biscuits and slices
anytime of the day for snacks or treats.

*Right: Pineapple and Muesli Cookies, Apricot
Date Slice, Pumpkin and Apricot Loaf
(all recipes page 66)*

65

dried FRUITS

Apricots, raisins, sultanas, currants, dates and figs are probably the most common dried fruits, but there are many others available which make an interesting addition to cakes, biscuits and slices. You might like to try dried pears or peaches in place of apricots.

❧ Fruits are dried either in the sun or by hot air.

❧ During the drying process the water content is concentrated and the flesh and skin darken.

❧ Dried fruits have a higher kilojoule/calorie, nutrient and sugar content than fresh fruit. The flavour and fibre content of fruit is also intensified when dried.

❧ Dried fruit is usually prewashed when you purchase it. However if you do need to wash the fruit before use, drain it well, spread it on a clean cloth and dry it in a low oven for 2-3 hours. If the fruit is not completely dry it will sink to the bottom of the cake.

❧ To prevent dried fruit from sinking to the bottom of a cake, toss it in a tablespoon of the flour used in the recipe before adding to the cake batter.

❧ Sugared or glacé fruits such as glacé cherries or pineapple should be rinsed and dried before using. This removes the sugary coating and helps to prevent the fruit from sinking.

❧ Store dried fruits in airtight containers at room temperature.

PINEAPPLE AND MUESLI COOKIES

Makes 30
Oven temperature 180°C, 350°F, Gas 4

- ☐ 2 cups/250 g/8 oz toasted muesli
- ☐ 1 cup/125 g/4 oz self-raising flour, sifted
- ☐ 1/2 cup/125 g/4 oz demerara sugar
- ☐ 45 g/1 1/2 oz glacé pineapple, chopped
- ☐ 125 g/4 oz butter, melted
- ☐ 1 egg, lightly beaten

1 Place muesli, flour, sugar and pineapple in a bowl. Add butter and egg and mix well to combine.
2 Place spoonfuls of mixture on greased baking trays and bake for 12-15 minutes or until golden brown. Stand on trays for 5 minutes before removing to wire racks to cool.

APRICOT DATE SLICE

Makes 30
Oven temperature 190°C, 375°F, Gas 5

- ☐ 90 g/3 oz dried apricots, chopped
- ☐ boiling water
- ☐ 2 cups/250 g/8 oz self-raising flour, sifted
- ☐ 1 cup/170 g/5 1/2 oz soft brown sugar
- ☐ 75 g/2 1/2 oz desiccated coconut
- ☐ 60 g/2 oz dates, chopped
- ☐ 185 g/6 oz butter, melted

LEMON ICING
- ☐ 90 g/3 oz butter, softened
- ☐ 1 1/2 cups/220 g/7 oz icing sugar, sifted
- ☐ 2 tablespoons lemon juice
- ☐ 15 g/1/2 oz desiccated coconut, toasted

1 Place apricots in a small bowl and add boiling water to cover. Set aside to soak for 10 minutes. Drain.
2 Sift together flour and sugar into a large mixing bowl. Add coconut, dates and apricots, pour in melted butter and mix to combine. Press mixture into a greased and lined, shallow 18 x 28 cm/7 x 11 in cake tin and bake for 25 minutes or until firm. Allow to cool in tin.
3 To make icing, place butter in a mixing bowl and beat until creamy. Add icing sugar and lemon juice and beat until icing is of a spreadable consistency. Add a little more lemon juice if necessary. Spread icing over cold slice and sprinkle with coconut. Cut into bars.

ELECTRIC MIXER

This appliance is invaluable for cake-making. It can be used for beating whole eggs or egg whites; beating egg yolks and sugar; creaming butter and sugar.

❧ As with all electric appliances you should read the manufacturer's handbook to ensure that you use the appliance correctly.

❧ During mixing you may need to stop the machine so that you can scrape down the sides of the bowl.

❧ When adding fruit and nuts to a mixture an electric mixer will help to distribute these more evenly, especially in heavier cakes.

❧ Beating and creaming can be done at higher speeds, however when adding heavier ingredients slower speeds should be used.

PUMPKIN AND APRICOT LOAF

Pumpkin gives a lovely moist texture to this delicious loaf.

Makes an 11 x 21 cm/4 1/2 x 8 1/2 in loaf
Oven temperature 180°C, 350°F, Gas 4

- ☐ 185 g/6 oz butter, softened
- ☐ 1 cup/170 g/5 1/2 oz soft brown sugar
- ☐ 1 teaspoon vanilla essence
- ☐ 2 eggs
- ☐ 1 cup/125 g/4 oz flour, sifted
- ☐ 1/2 cup/60 g/2 oz self-raising flour, sifted
- ☐ 1 teaspoon ground nutmeg
- ☐ 1/2 teaspoon ground cinnamon
- ☐ 300 g/9 1/2 oz pumpkin, cooked and mashed
- ☐ 125 g/4 oz dried apricots, chopped

1 Place butter, sugar and vanilla essence in a large mixing bowl and beat until light and creamy. Add eggs one at a time, beating well after each addition. Sift together flour and self-raising flour, nutmeg and cinnamon. Mix flour mixture and pumpkin, alternately, into butter mixture, then fold in apricots.
2 Spoon batter into a greased and lined 11 x 21 cm/4 1/2 x 8 1/2 in loaf tin and bake for 1 hour or until cooked when tested with a skewer.

HONEY OAT LOAF

Plain, or spread with a little butter and jam, this loaf tastes delicious.

Makes an 11 x 21 cm/4^1/$_2$ x 8^1/$_2$ in loaf
Oven temperature 180°C, 350°F, Gas 4

- ☐ ^{1}/$_2$ cup/60 g/2 oz flour
- ☐ 1 cup/125 g/4 oz self-raising flour
- ☐ 1 teaspoon salt
- ☐ 1^1/$_2$ teaspoons baking powder
- ☐ 1 cup/90 g/3 oz rolled oats
- ☐ 45 g/1^1/$_2$ oz butter, melted
- ☐ 2 eggs, lightly beaten
- ☐ ^{1}/$_4$ cup/60 mL/2 fl oz water
- ☐ ^{1}/$_2$ cup/170 g/5^1/$_2$ oz honey, warmed

1   Sift together flour and self-raising flour, salt and baking powder into a large mixing bowl. Stir in rolled oats.

2   Combine butter, eggs, water and honey and mix into flour mixture until just combined. Pour into a greased and lined 11 x 21 cm/4^1/$_2$ x 8^1/$_2$ in loaf tin and bake for 40-45 minutes or until cooked when tested with a skewer. Stand in tin for 5 minutes before turning onto a wire rack to cool completely.

Honey Oat Loaf

BAKER'S KITCHEN

Pinwheel biscuits always look impressive and are very easy to make. Just follow the step-by-step instructions for making these delicious biscuits that wrap a spiced dough around a wonderful fig and almond filling.

FIG PINWHEEL BISCUITS

Makes 50
Oven temperature 180°C, 350°F, Gas 4

- [ ] **170 g/5^1/2 oz butter**
- [ ] **1 cup/170 g/5^1/2 oz soft brown sugar**
- [ ] **1 egg**
- [ ] **^{1}/2 teaspoon vanilla essence**
- [ ] **3 cups/375 g/12 oz flour**
- [ ] **^{1}/2 teaspoon bicarbonate of soda**
- [ ] **^{1}/4 teaspoon ground cinnamon**
- [ ] **^{1}/4 teaspoon ground nutmeg**
- [ ] **2 tablespoons milk**

FIG AND ALMOND FILLING
- [ ] **250 g/8 oz dried figs, finely chopped**
- [ ] **^{1}/4 cup/60 g/2 oz sugar**
- [ ] **^{1}/2 cup/125 mL/4 fl oz water**
- [ ] **^{1}/4 teaspoon ground mixed spice**
- [ ] **30 g/1 oz almonds, finely chopped**

1 To make filling, place figs, sugar, water and mixed spice in a saucepan and bring to the boil. Reduce heat and cook, stirring, for 2-3 minutes or until mixture is thick. Remove from heat and stir in almonds. Set aside to cool.

2 Place butter in a large mixing bowl and beat until light and fluffy. Gradually add sugar, beating well after each addition until mixture is creamy. Beat in egg and vanilla essence.

3 Sift together flour, bicarbonate of soda, cinnamon and nutmeg. Beat milk and half the flour mixture into butter mixture. Stir in remaining flour mixture. Turn dough onto a lightly floured surface and knead lightly. Roll into a ball, wrap in plastic food wrap and refrigerate for 30 minutes.

4 Divide dough into two portions. Roll one portion out to a 20 x 28 cm/8 x 11 in rectangle and spread with filling. Roll up from the long side, like a Swiss roll. Repeat with remaining dough and filling. Wrap rolls in plastic food wrap and refrigerate for 15 minutes or until you are ready to cook the biscuits.

5 Cut rolls into 1 cm/^{1}/2 in slices. Place slices on greased baking trays and cook for 10-12 minutes. Stand biscuits on trays for 1 minute before removing to a wire rack to cool completely.

Freeze it: The uncooked rolls can be frozen if you wish. When you have unexpected guests or the biscuit barrel is empty, these biscuits are great standbys.

Divide dough into two portions. Roll one portion out to a 20 x 28 cm/8 x 11 in rectangle and spread with filling.

Roll dough up from the long side, like a Swiss roll. Wrap rolls in plastic food wrap.

Cut rolls into 1 cm/^{1}/2 in slices and place on greased baking trays.

BRAN DATE LOAF

Makes an 11 x 21 cm/4^1/$_2$ x 8^1/$_2$ in loaf
Oven temperature 190°C, 375°F, Gas 5

- ☐ **2 cups/250 g/8 oz self-raising flour**
- ☐ **^{1}/$_4$ teaspoon ground cinnamon**
- ☐ **^{1}/$_4$ teaspoon ground nutmeg**
- ☐ **1 teaspoon bicarbonate of soda**
- ☐ **^{1}/$_4$ cup/45 g/1^1/$_2$ oz sugar**
- ☐ **60 g/2 oz butter**
- ☐ **1 cup/45 g/1^1/$_2$ oz unprocessed bran**
- ☐ **1 egg, beaten**
- ☐ **1 cup/250 mL/8 fl oz milk**
- ☐ **185 g/6 oz dates, chopped**

1 Place flour, cinnamon, nutmeg, bicarbonate of soda and sugar in a food processor and process to combine. Add butter and bran and process for 1 minute longer.

2 Combine egg and milk and stir into bran mixture with dates. Spoon batter into a greased and lined 11 x 21 cm/ 4^1/$_2$ x 8^1/$_2$ in loaf tin and bake for 50-55 minutes or until cooked when tested with a skewer. Stand in tin for 5 minutes before turning onto a wire rack to cool.

BRAN AND PEANUT COOKIES

Makes 45
Oven temperature 180°C, 350°F, Gas 4

- ☐ **4 cups/185 g/6 oz bran flakes, crumbled**
- ☐ **2 cups/250 g/8 oz flour, sifted**
- ☐ **^{1}/$_2$ cup/90 g/3 oz soft brown sugar**
- ☐ **75 g/2^1/$_2$ oz unsalted roasted peanuts**
- ☐ **^{1}/$_2$ cup/125 g/4 oz smooth peanut butter**
- ☐ **^{1}/$_2$ cup/170 g/5^1/$_2$ oz honey, warmed**
- ☐ **185 g/6 oz butter, melted**
- ☐ **2 eggs, lightly beaten**

1 Place bran flakes, flour, sugar and peanuts in a large mixing bowl. Combine peanut butter, honey, butter and eggs and stir in bran mixture. Mix well to combine.

2 Place spoonfuls of mixture 2.5 cm/1 in apart on greased baking trays. Bake for 10-12 minutes or until lightly browned. Allow to cool on trays.

Rock Cakes, Carrot Cake

Floral ornament Home & Garden

CARROT CAKE

A gluten-free cake that is suitable for anyone who has a wheat intolerance.

Makes a 20 cm/8 in square cake
Oven temperature 180°C, 350°F, Gas 4

- ☐ **2 cups/375 g/2 oz ground rice, sifted**
- ☐ **2 teaspoons ground mixed spice**
- ☐ **2 teaspoons bicarbonate of soda**
- ☐ **1 cup/170 g/5^1/2 oz soft brown sugar**
- ☐ **125 g/4 oz margarine, softened**
- ☐ **4 small carrots, grated**
- ☐ **125 g/4 oz pecans, chopped**
- ☐ **170 g/5^1/2 oz sultanas**
- ☐ **2 cups/400 g/12^1/2 oz natural low-fat yogurt**
- ☐ **1 teaspoon vanilla essence**
- ☐ **icing sugar**

1 Place ground rice, mixed spice, bicarbonate of soda, brown sugar, margarine, carrots, pecans, sultanas, yogurt and vanilla essence in a large mixing bowl and mix well to combine all ingredients.

2 Spoon mixture into a greased and lined 20 cm/8 in square cake tin and bake for 45-50 minutes or until cooked when tested with a skewer. Stand cake in tin for 10 minutes before turning onto a wire rack to cool. Dust with icing sugar.

ROCK CAKES

Makes 30
Oven temperature 180°C, 350°F, Gas 4

- ☐ **2 cups/250 g/8 oz self-raising flour, sifted**
- ☐ **^{1}/4 cup/60 g/2 oz caster sugar**
- ☐ **90 g/3 oz butter**
- ☐ **125 g/4 oz mixed dried fruit, chopped**
- ☐ **1 teaspoon finely grated lemon rind**
- ☐ **1 teaspoon finely grated orange rind**
- ☐ **1 egg, lightly beaten**
- ☐ **^{1}/3 cup/90 mL/3 fl oz milk**
- ☐ **^{1}/2 teaspoon cinnamon mixed with 2 tablespoons caster sugar**

1 Place flour and sugar in a mixing bowl. Rub in butter, using fingertips, until mixture resembles fine bread crumbs. Stir in mixed fruit, lemon rind and orange rind. Add egg and milk and mix to form a soft dough.

2 Place tablespoons of mixture on greased baking trays and dust lightly with cinnamon sugar mixture. Bake for 12-15 minutes or until golden. Transfer to wire racks to cool.

Bran and Peanut Cookies, Bran Date Loaf

NO-BAKE

No-bake biscuits and slices are ideal quick and easy treats. They are also suitable for those days when the kids want to get into the kitchen.

Right: Rocky Road Slice (page 74),
Mango Cheesecake Slice, Corn Flake
Crunchies
(recipes page 75)

CRUSHING BISCUITS

🍃 Place biscuits in a food processor or blender and using the pulse button process the biscuits until crumbs are the required size.

🍃 Place biscuits in a freezer bag, seal and roll over or pound with a rolling pin until crumbs are the required size.

🍃 Place biscuits between two pieces of baking or greaseproof paper and roll over with a rolling pin, pushing biscuits to the centre of the paper occasionally, until crumbs are the required size.

ROCKY ROAD SLICE

In this delicious indulgence, Rocky Road, an all-time favourite, is made into a slice with a chocolate biscuit base.

Makes 24 bars

☐ **200 g/6^1/$_2$ oz plain chocolate biscuits, crushed**
☐ **125 g/4 oz butter, melted**

ROCKY ROAD TOPPING
☐ **300 g/9^1/$_2$ oz chocolate, melted and cooled**
☐ **100 g/3^1/$_2$ oz white marshmallows, halved**
☐ **100 g/3^1/$_2$ oz pink marshmallows, halved**
☐ **45 g/1^1/$_2$ oz desiccated coconut**
☐ **3 tablespoons crushed nuts**

1 Place crushed biscuits and butter in a bowl and mix well to combine. Press mixture into a greased and lined, shallow 18 x 28 cm/7 x 11 in cake tin. Refrigerate for 10-15 minutes until firm.

2 To make topping, place chocolate, white and pink marshmallows, coconut and nuts in a bowl and mix to combine. Pour over base and refrigerate until firm. Cut into bars.

Chocolate Cherry Slice,
Caramel Crunch Slice

CARAMEL CRUNCH SLICE

Makes 36 triangles

- ☐ **200 g/6$^{1}/_{2}$ oz plain biscuits, crushed**
- ☐ **125 g/4 oz butter, melted**

CARAMEL CRUNCH TOPPING
- ☐ **1 cup/250 mL/8 fl oz sweetened condensed milk**
- ☐ **$^{1}/_{4}$ cup/90 g/3 oz golden syrup**
- ☐ **90 g/3 oz butter, chopped**
- ☐ **$^{1}/_{2}$ cup/90 g/3 oz soft brown sugar**
- ☐ **1$^{1}/_{2}$ cups/45 g/1$^{1}/_{2}$ oz unsweetened puffed rice cereal**

1   Place crushed biscuits and butter into a bowl and mix to combine. Press into a greased and lined, shallow 18 x 28 cm/7 x 11 in cake tin and refrigerate until firm.
2   To make topping, place condensed milk, golden syrup, butter, and brown sugar in a saucepan and cook, stirring, over a low heat until smooth. Bring to the boil and cook for 5 minutes, stirring constantly. Stir in rice cereal and pour over base. Refrigerate until firm. Cut into triangles.

MANGO CHEESECAKE SLICE

Makes 28 squares

- ☐ **60 g/2 oz packaged plain biscuits**

MANGO TOPPING
- ☐ **250 g/8 oz cream cheese**
- ☐ **$^{1}/_{2}$ cup/100 g/3$^{1}/_{2}$ oz caster sugar**
- ☐ **440 g/14 oz canned mangoes, drained**
- ☐ **300 mL/9$^{1}/_{2}$ fl oz cream (double)**
- ☐ **6 teaspoons gelatine dissolved in $^{1}/_{3}$ cup/90 mL/3 fl oz hot water, cooled**
- ☐ **2 tablespoons passion fruit pulp**

1   To make topping, place cream cheese, sugar, mangoes, cream and gelatine mixture in a food processor and process until smooth. Stir in passion fruit pulp.
2   Line a shallow 18 x 28 cm/7 x 11 in cake tin with aluminium foil and place biscuits over the base. Trim biscuits to fit tin if necessary.
3   Pour topping over biscuits and refrigerate until firm. Cut into squares.

CORN FLAKE CRUNCHIES

Makes 40

- ☐ **125 g/4 oz butter**
- ☐ **$^{1}/_{3}$ cup/125 g/4 oz golden syrup**
- ☐ **4 cups/185 g/6 oz corn flakes**
- ☐ **30 g/1 oz shredded coconut**
- ☐ **90 g/3 oz chocolate chips**
- ☐ **60 g/2 oz pecans, chopped**

1   Place butter and golden syrup in a small saucepan and cook, stirring, over a low heat until butter is melted, then simmer for 3-4 minutes until mixture is thick and syrupy.
2   Place corn flakes, coconut, chocolate chips, and pecans in a large bowl. Pour in syrup and mix to combine. Place spoonfuls of mixture in paper patty cases and refrigerate until set.

CHOCOLATE CHERRY SLICE

Makes 40

- ☐ **200 g/6$^{1}/_{2}$ oz dark chocolate, melted**

CHERRY COCONUT TOPPING
- ☐ **$^{1}/_{2}$ cup/125 mL/4 fl oz sweetened condensed milk**
- ☐ **140 g/5$^{1}/_{2}$ oz desiccated coconut**
- ☐ **2 tablespoons icing sugar**
- ☐ **100 g/3$^{1}/_{2}$ oz red glacé cherries, finely chopped**

1   Line a deep 23 cm/9 in square cake tin with nonstick baking paper. Spread chocolate evenly over base of tin and refrigerate until set.
2   To make topping, place condensed milk, coconut, icing sugar and cherries in a bowl and mix well to combine. Spread over base and refrigerate until set. Cut into bars.

notes on SHORTENING

Fat or shortening in whatever form makes a cake tender and helps improve the keeping quality.

❧ Good quality margarine and butter usually are interchangeable.

❧ In most cases fats should be at room temperature for cake and biscuit making.

❧ To allow hard shortenings to soften, stand at room temperature for an hour before using.

❧ If using a soft margarine high in polyunsaturated fats, use it straight from the refrigerator.

❧ Oil is sometimes used in baked products. This is a lighter alternative to butter or margarine and is often used in recipes for carrot cake.

❧ If using an oil for making a cake choose one that has a mild flavour. Corn and vegetable oils are good choices. Never use olive oil or other strong-flavoured oil or your cake will have an unpleasant flavour.

❧ Butter absorbs other smells easily, so when keeping it in the refrigerator make sure that it is covered and away from ingredients such as onions and fish or you will have a strong-smelling butter that can affect the taste of baked goods.

❧ Butter keeps well in the freezer for up to three months, if well wrapped.

❧ As oils have a tendency to turn rancid quickly they should be stored away from heat and light. The refrigerator is a good place to store oils. You will find that some oils go cloudy and semi-solid when stored in the refrigerator, but will quickly revert to their original state when left at room temperature for a short time.

THE RIGHT TOOLS

Turn the page and you will find an easy guide to make sure that you have the right tools for the job.

THE RIGHT TOOLS KEY

1   Swiss roll tin
2   Shallow cake tin
3   Lemon squeezer
4   20 cm/8 in square cake tin
5   Kitchen scales
6   20 cm/8 in round cake tin
7   Food processor
8   Flour sifter
9   Rolling pin
10 Fluted cake tin
11 23 cm/9 in ring tin
12 20 cm/8 in sandwich tins
13 Muffin tins
14 Flan tin with removable base
15 Hand-held electric mixer
16 Grater
17 250 mL/8 fl oz measuring jug
18 Mixing bowls
19 Wire cooling rack
20 Loaf tins
21 Pastry brush
22 Wooden spoon
23 Metal spatula
24 Serrated knife
25 Palette knife
26 Paper patty cases
27 Piping bag
28 Piping nozzles
29 Measuring cups
30 Measuring spoons
31 Balloon whisk
32 Wooden spatula
33 Rubber spatula
34 Sieve
35 Nonstick baking paper
36 Oven mitt

INDEX